# 21 Days
# To A New Path

## A Guidebook for Anyone Seeking to Change Old Behavioral Patterns

### DR. CHRISTIAN CONTE

ISBN:

# DEDICATION

To everyone who reads this book: May the words in these pages help guide you to becoming the best version of yourself.

*In the field of personal transformation, gurus seek to guide others, whereas masters seek to guide themselves. You are the only person you will always live with, so get to know yourself, and then pursue mastering the only person you will ever have control over: Yourself.*

## ACKNOWLEDGMENTS

I would like to thank Secretary John Wetzel for giving me the opportunity to impact the Pennsylvania Department of Corrections. I would like to thank everyone I encountered in the space of corrections, from my center in South Lake Tahoe, CA, to the PA DOC, to the GA DOC, and to the local, state, and national leaders who strive constantly to make prison a place for people to train to become the best version of themselves. I am most grateful to my wife and daughter: My family gives me the strength that I in turn am able to share with others.

# Worth Understanding....

The exercises you're about to do can absolutely help you change your life.

The material in these pages has been used to help countless people radically transform their lives in extremely positive ways.

But NONE of this material – and not even all the science in the world – will do ANYTHING for you until YOU take control and change your life.

**This entire program ultimately boils down to the effort you put into it.**

Not one thing that any of us has ever done (good, bad or indifferent) can be changed. And when it comes to what really counts *right now*: Nothing we have ever done in the past matters. ***The only thing that matters right now is what any of us do from this moment forward***.

# From: *"You tell me what to do,"*
# To: *"Here is who I've become"*

There is more than one way to be incarcerated. Some people are physically free but mentally incarcerated; others are mentally free but physically incarcerated. And some are both imprisoned physically and in their own minds. Remember: Where you've been, what you've done, or even what you know will never matter as much as what you do now and from this moment forward.

In the past, *many incarcerated individuals have asked about what classes and programs they "need" to take to be considered for release*. In short, their old approach has been, "What do I need to do?" In this approach, however, that question will no longer be helpful to ask, as the new question that will be the central focus of the rest of your incarceration is, "Who will I become?" Therefore, before you are freed, whether it is from a mental or physical prison (or both), and whether or not you encounter a literal or metaphorical parole board, the focus of your assessment will not be on what classes and programs you took, not on what books you read, videos you watched or what you say you "know," but the focus of the assessment will be entirely on **who you have become**.

The singular goal for you during this incarceration is to become the best possible version of yourself, including mastering your self-control, decision-making, goal setting, follow-through, personal responsibility, and accountability. In that sense, everything in these pages is for you to use to train to become the best version of yourself. Even the greatest champion fighters train for every fight they have. And like a fighter preparing for a championship fight, this incarceration is "training" for you to win the greatest fight of your life: Your life!

In the end, **you will be asked to demonstrate with your actions how you apply what you learn in your everyday life**, and you will be assessed accordingly. In your final evaluation, you will be asked to describe who you have become, including citing concrete examples.

*If nothing changes, nothing changes.*

# The Spirit of Change

Change is the only constant in life. There is a great Zen saying that you cannot step in the same spot in a river twice (because the second time you'd be stepping into new waters). As humans, we often cringe at change because we tend to be creatures of habit. But growth occurs in change.

If you walk the same distance on the same path, you will get to the same destination. It is foolish for any of us to walk the same distance on the same path and expect to magically arrive at a new destination. In a similar way, if you do the same things you've always done, you will continue to get the same results you have always gotten. If you want different results in your life, you have to do different things.

Personal growth is all about change. People talk a lot about prison reform - about changing the system of incarceration and about the changes that need to happen. People have talked about it for so long, and I think that they got used to talking about; so much so that many don't realize that it is actually here. It is in your hands right now. This 21-day program is prison reform. It is a path to mental and physical freedom.

Now, that doesn't mean that you run around telling people that you "completed the 21-day program, so they should... (fill in the blank). Instead, it's about living the changes that you make from doing this program every single day of your life. It's not about an end-goal, it's about the process of becoming. It's about showing the world with your actions day in and day out that you are a different person. And the reason why this is actual prison reform? Well, for the first time in the history of corrections, the stated goal is not about completing X, Y or Z to be free; instead, this entire incarceration is now about who you will become.

Real change doesn't happen when you seek to *tell* people about the changes that you make or insist that they see them. It happens when you show them. If a person needs to convince, threaten, coerce or intimidate others to see the changes he or she's made, then that person hasn't changed. Again, taking the same path the same distance and expecting to be in a different place is foolish.

That is why you will know that you have made real changes when you live as the best version of yourself every single day, regardless of who ever knows about who you've become. The changes that you make will likely be subtle and happen over time. You will notice the changes you make long before anyone else, because people see your actions, not your intentions. People can't see your thoughts, just as you cannot see theirs. And just as you judge others on their actions, but judge yourself on your intentions, others do the same, too. So it will take time for others to notice the changes you make, and you will not have to "tell" anyone about how you're different, because when you're different for long enough, others will notice.

This program is designed to bring the best out of you. It's designed to help you constantly change and grow. The questions, the exercises, the focus on all aspects of your life... all of this material is geared toward you fulfilling your potential and helping you to become the best version of yourself.

So let's start with who you were, and let's compare it to who you want to become.

**Who I was:**

**Who I am becoming:**

*Be mindful that the changes you make will take time for others to see.*

# Why Living Your Message Matters

Once an inmate complained angrily to a teacher about the parole board. He said, "Those people only meet with us for what amounts to be minutes, so how the Hell can they claim to know anything about us after only listening to us for a couple minutes? It's so messed up! There's no way they can tell anything about us in a few minutes!" And the teacher asked, "When you say it like that, it doesn't seem like they could know much," to which the inmate replied, "Exactly!"

So the teacher looked at the floor as if to think for a moment, then looked back at the inmate and asked, "But do you *know* that they don't know you after only a couple minutes?" And the inmate said, "Oh I know!" He continued. He said, "I've seen these kinds of people my whole life. I can just tell who's not open as soon as I see them." The teacher said, "How do you know that they're not open?" And the inmate replied, "I just know. I've lived this for my whole life. I can look at them and tell instantly." To which the teacher said, "So, you can read them in seconds, and you're certain that that's how they are?" And this time the inmate clapped his hands three times at the teacher and said, "Yes. I'm telling you, I have too much experience. I can see it in a second!" The teacher paused, and then he looked the inmate in the eyes and said with compassion, "If you know that your experiences have taught you how to read others in seconds – if you know that there are little tells, signs, and things people say that help you read them so quickly, then what makes you believe that the parole board members can't do the same when it comes to you?"

The inmate's face dropped. He fumbled for what to say, and then, in an incredibly mature way (because it takes tremendous maturity to question our own convictions), he said, "You're right. I never thought about it that way. I guess if I'm certain that I know about them, then they can be certain that they know about me." The teacher, with tremendous compassion, said, "That's incredible that you are able to be that open to learning. It's important, too, to understand that even though there is always more to everyone than we ever immediately see, it's also true that there are things that people say and do that give us a very large window into their lives.

**Just as easily as you can read others, others can read you, too.**

# Self-Assessment 1: Behind the Curtain

**The following questions offer you a glimpse into the mindset of what will shape your next assessment. You will notice that the questions center on not only what you've learned, but specifically on behavioral examples that support what you say. In other words, it is no longer enough to say *what* you've learned, you must also be able to give practical examples of how you have implemented what you report learning.**

What have you learned over the last six months of your life?

_____

_____

How are you different from five years ago (Give specific examples of how you have applied what you have learned over the last 5 years.)

_____

_____

What obstacles have you encountered that stand out to you?

_____

_____

How did you succeed or fail in attempting to overcome those obstacles? (Give specific examples of times that you have succeeded and specific examples of times that you have failed.)

_____

_____

What did you learn from those experiences?

_____

_____

Give concrete examples of how you have applied what you learned from those experiences to future situations?

_____

_____

Give an example of the most recent time that impulse control got the best of you.

_____

_____

Give an example of the most recent time that you were able to delay or even resist an impulse?

_____

_____

What specifically have you learned about impulses and how to handle them?

_____

_____

Give an example of your most recent conflict, and describe how you handled it.

_____

_____

Compare how you handled this most recent conflict with how you have handled conflicts in the past.

_____

_____

What specifically have you learned about conflict and how you handle anger?

_____

_____

Give an example of what your inner dialogue looks like around anger.

_____

_____

What are your goals in life?

_____

_____

What specifically do you do to pursue those goals?

_____

_____

What does your daily schedule look like?

_____

_____

What healthy habits do you practice, and how regularly or infrequently do you practice them?

_____

_____

What poor habits do you practice, and how regularly or infrequently do you practice them?

_____

_____

What obstacles are likely to cause you the most challenges in the future?

_____

_____

What skills do you intend to use to get around those obstacles, and how have you used those specific skills to overcome a similar obstacle already?

_____

_____

What insight do you have about yourself now that you did not have before?

_____

_____

_____

_____

_____

_____

_____

_____

_____

**(Be mindful to track the way you experience these questions the first time you encounter them so that you can compare them to the end of the 21 days, and again in the future.)**

# Preparing for Life Outside:
# "Doing Time" Versus "Living"

How you spend time during incarceration is up to you. The phrase "doing time" suggests that you are just biding your time until enough years go by; and if that is what you choose to do, then it's important to know that the consequences of that are that you will not likely change your thoughts, behaviors or habits. That also means that when you leave your prison, you will likely do the same things you have always done. Simply "doing time" leads people to coming back to prison. "Doing time," after all, is no different than just being put in a timeout; but instead of parents or others putting you in a timeout, when you choose to just bide your time in life, you put yourself in a timeout.

The choice is always yours as to whether or not you want to use your time wisely or just "do time."

On the outside of physical prisons, people are "living" their lives and, whether they fully appreciate it or not, are experiencing their freedom. But every inmate in prison knows as well as anyone, however, that when you are in prison, your life doesn't stop. You are very much alive, and you continue to experience your own life every single second of every single day. The question you have to face, however, is: **How are you using your time every day?** Because if you dedicate your every moment in prison to learning, growing, and practicing new habits, then you will significantly increase your chance of living out your potential when you are released from prison.

The more accurate description of your life is that "living" has already started for you, but it is you who can choose to put personal growth on hold and just "do time." It is also you, who can be wise about the way you spend every moment of your incarceration. If you have any shot of truly being free, then it's extremely important for you to understand that, "if nothing changes, then nothing changes." In other words, you cannot live as you always have and rationally demand that the world gives you different results.

Your actual behaviors are going to be evaluated at some point before your freedom occurs. That moment of assessment, whether it's in front of a parole board or the mirror, can be viewed as either an "opportunity" or as a "barrier." When you get to an exit meeting, for example, *you are faced head on with describing how you have spent your time in prison.* If you have just "done time," then the reality is that you haven't done enough time, and you will likely "get a hit." If you have worked hard every single day of your incarceration on improving yourself physically, mentally, emotionally, and spiritually, then any meeting about what you're ready to experience will be an opportunity, not a barrier for your freedom.

Whether you "do time" or "live" is ultimately up to you. It's never too late to start living. People who try to get over on authority and try to just say what they believe people who are in charge want to hear look about as foolish as a toddler who covers his eyes and thinks no one can see him. **People are seeing your actions, not your intentions or promises**. You cannot fool anyone on this: Most importantly, however, you cannot fool yourself. My advice is for you to choose to live, because your life has already started….

Imagine that you have to sit in front of a parole board before you can be free. Here are some concepts that, if truly understood, would greatly increase your chance of having a successful meeting:

• Preparing for your exit meeting is something that you do from the first moment of your incarceration.

• If you believe that you can "just tell people what they want to hear," then you are vastly missing the fact that there is nothing that anyone "wants to hear," and that anyone who is evaluating whether you have made actual behavioral changes since the start of your incarceration is looking solely at your actions, and not at your words at all.

• General statements, such as "*I realized I needed to change…*" or "*I learned that every crime has a victim…*" or "*I learned that mindset is important…*" are absolutely meaningless **_unless you can describe specifically how those statements literally apply to you_**. Without specifics, general statements demonstrate that you are trying to "just say what you think others want to hear," and that is a form of manipulation – so using general statements without specifics demonstrates that you have most likely just "done time," versus having used your time to grow.

• If you cannot talk about what you have learned specifically, then you have not learned it. We can all, for example, sit in a chair and be physically present for a lecture on quantum science, but just being present for such a talk doesn't make us physicists. Likewise, you can be physically present for things like drug and alcohol classes or parenting classes, but if you cannot demonstrate *how* you have applied the information directly to your life, then it is no different than sitting in on a physics lecture and expecting to magically be a physicist afterwards.

• Do not talk to parole, authorities, or anyone else about what you "intend to do in the future" if you have not already started working on it. For example, if you say, "I intend to go to school to be a drug and alcohol counselor," that's a noble goal to pursue, but if you haven't read books on drug and alcohol counseling while you were incarcerated, then saying that you have that goal has no credibility or believability at all. There is a tremendous amount of time to read in prison, and there is no excuse for not being well read in the subject area that you claim you hope to pursue.

• Don't make the over-used statement that you "think about your family," or that you "love your kids," because the fact is, it's pretty normal for people to think about their family or love their children. In fact, it would be strange not to do so. Although your family might be on your mind, for that statement to hold any weight, you would need to back it up with examples of how you have specifically made behavioral changes with your "family on your mind" while you've been incarcerated, otherwise, those type of *general* statements about family or children come across as an attempt to "play the victim" and elicit sympathy from the board.

• Your body language speaks volumes about your attitude. If you walk into an evaluation meeting with parole (or any type of authorities) with the same type of nonchalant body language you would have to sit around and loaf, then you are demonstrating with your body language that you don't value the significance of the opportunity to meet with the people who are taking time to evaluate where you are.

• As easy as it is for you to spot someone who is a fake, it's equally as easy for parole, authority figures, your loved ones, and others to see people who are obviously saying one thing but living entirely differently. If you don't live the message that you are saying, then other people will most definitely see that. Conversely, if you *do* live the message that you are delivering to them, then they will see that, as well.

In the space below, write down any additional thoughts that you believe can help you prepare for your exit out of prison and become truly free:

_____

_____

_____

_____

_____

_____

*I won't say "good luck" to you, because "luck" implies that random forces outside of yourself will be the key to you changing. My statement to you instead is: "**Good understanding**;" because the more you understand about why you do what you do, and the more you understand the tools you need to be the best possible version of yourself, the more likely you are to succeed.*

# Vision

Visualize clearly what you want to achieve. The more clearly you visualize what you want, the more likely you are to get it. Take the time to really see exactly what you want in life. See the path to get there. See the obstacles, but more importantly, see the path you can take to get around those obstacles.

# Hard Work

Work harder than you ever have. Push yourself to work hard even when no one notices. NFL legend Ray Lewis once said: "Wins and losses are a dime a dozen, but effort? Nobody can just that, because effort is between you and you." Only you know what your best effort looks like, but also, the Navy seals operate on the 40% rule. The 40% rule is that when you have pushed yourself to complete exhaustion and you have the thought that you don't have any more to give, well, you're only at 40% of what you can actually do. You still have 60% more to give. The point? You are more capable than you realize.

# Patience

Have patience. Big changes in life are absolutely possible, but they take time. Keep going, even when it's difficult. Keep working hard. Keep visualizing exactly what you want, keep working on having self-control even when things aren't going the way you want them to be going, and practice the kind of patience that you want to master.

**When you master practicing vision, hard work and patience, your life changes profoundly.**

# ASK YOURSELF EVERY DAY:

**PERSONAL GROWTH**

- In what ways does my ego stop me from growing as a person?
- What am I doing today to gain new insights about myself?
- What kinds of habits do I practice daily that help me grow as a person?

**EDUCATION**

- What am I studying right now that's helping me learn more about the world in which I live?
- What books am I reading right now?
- Is what I'm reading right now helping me master a field of study that I want to master?

**INNER PEACE**

- What daily habits am I practicing currently that help me master my own mind?
- Are the thoughts that I allow to dominate my mind the kind of thoughts that I want to dominate my mind?
- What kind of thoughts would lead me to experiencing the type of inner peace I hope to experience?

**LEGACY**

- What actions am I doing right now that will contribute to the kind of legacy that I want to leave in this world?
- Am I putting others' needs before my own, or am I still caught up in needing to have whatever my impulses want?
- What positive legacy do I hope to leave in this world from this moment forward?

**You master what you practice.**

# THE YES-BUT GAME

You have way more answers inside you than you permit yourself to listen to. For years, you have had an inner voice directing you to do what you know is best for you, and then somehow, you end up not doing what you know is best. The reason? Oftentimes we play the "yes-but" game with ourselves. The "Yes-but" game occurs anytime we agree or say "yes" to a valid point that others make about us, and then follow that agreement or "yes" with a "but," and then go on to justify why we did what we did or do what we do.

The yes-but game enables us to avoid changing, because we give ourselves excuses to keep doing what we've always done. The yes-but game might be one of the single biggest barriers to people changing, because it allows people say that they "know" whatever is being said, but it gives them the excuse to keep doing things wrong.

**Examples of the Yes-But game:**

"Yes, I know I should work on myself, but I would rather talk about how everyone else needs to change."

"Yes, I know it's important for me to avoid making excuses, but if I don't make excuses, then I will have to put effort into changing, and I don't feel like doing that, because it's easier to just point out other people's flaws."

"Yes, I know it's not good for me to do the same things I've always done, and yes, I know that 'doing the same thing you've always done and expecting a different result is the definition of insanity,' but, it's way easier for me to not have to change, so I'm gonna keep doing what I've always done."

"Yes, technically I know I'm not owed anything in life, but I'm gonna still demand things from others, because even though I say I'm not owed anything in life, I actually believe I'm owed lots of things."

To defeat the "yes-but" game, it is extremely important to be able to identify and call yourself on any excuses you make. To begin that awareness, let's start by identifying what types of excuses you have tended to use throughout your life.
Let's start by taking a hard look at how you have used the yes-but game to sabotage your own path in the past.

These are the most common types of excuses I have used throughout my life to justify why I do what I do:

_____

_____

_____

_____

Obviously when I make excuses, others can see what I'm doing more clearly than I believe they can see, so if I step back and analyze my actions, I see that these are the things that others see in me when I am using excuses:

_____

_____

_____

_____

Now let's look at some truths that you want to live your life by without making any excuses. In the following space, write down the types of things that you want to live by moving forward (in other words, these are statements that you know to be true, or the "Yes" part of the yes-but game).

_____

_____

_____

_____

The more we make ourselves and others aware of the excuses we tend to make, the more prepared we are to change our behaviors and no longer rely on those excuses anymore. The less prepared we are to make real changes in our lives, the more likely we are to downplay, minimize or outright deny the kinds of excuses we make. In other words, the only reason a person is unable or unwilling to identify the excuses he tends to use is that he is still actively trying to get away with using those excuses.

## Turning "Yes-But" into "Yes, and here's how I will change...."

Describe a typical "yes-but" statement that you've used in the past, and then restate the same statement in a way that allows you to be genuinely follow through with doing what you know to be right.

_____

_____

_____

_____

_____

_____

## Self-evaluation:

What are you taking away from doing this exercise?

_____

_____

How will you (or won't you) apply this lesson to your life right now?

_____

_____

What behavioral examples can you site from your life that can show that you are actually applying this concept?

_____

_____

**Personal growth is personal; that's why our egos take it so personally.**

# Cartoon World Versus the Real World

There is a difference between what I call the cartoon world and the real world. The **cartoon world is** comprised of **the way we believe the world should be**, and **the real world is the way the world actually is**. The more you expect the world to be the way you think it "should" be, the less you live in reality, and the more disappointed you tend to be. The world does not operate the way you think it "should," it operates the way it actually does. The more you can recognize when you're in the cartoon world, the better chance you have to step away from it and align your expectations with the reality that's right in front of you.

1.  This is the way I think the world *should* be:

   _____

   _____

2.  Here is how I would be if the world worked out exactly the way I think it should:

   _____

   _____

3.  This is the way the world actually is, however:

   _____

   _____

4.  And here is how it's best for me to be in the world the way it actually is:

   _____

   _____

## Iron Sharpens Iron: When Friends Push Each Other to Grow

"It *shouldn't* be like this," said a man who was stuck in his cartoon world.

"But it *is* like this," said his friend (who operated in the real world).

"But it *shouldn't* be," said the first man.

"But it is," said his friend.

"So we should just accept it?" asked the first.

"What's the alternative?" asked his friend.

"To work to change it," declared the first.

"Well that's a different thing altogether," said his friend. And then he continued: "Working to change how things are begins by accepting how things are. When you accept the reality of what is *actually* occurring, then you can work to make real change happen. But if you spend your time talking about how things "should" or "shouldn't" be, then you are just speaking about a make-believe world in your own mind where people and the world operate according to your magical, untrue thoughts. But when you accept the reality of what is actually happening, then everything you do will impact the world the way it is."

"I understand that," said the first man. And from that moment forward, the man who was previously stuck in his cartoon world became very accurate in the way he spoke.

**Personal Challenge:** Find someone around you who will challenge you on your cartoon world thoughts and push you to be accurate in your language.

## Applying the concept of the cartoon world / real world to your life:

Let's say that you're in a prison cell and a corrections officer says something that you believe he "shouldn't" have said, you have options with how you can reply. In this exercise, take some time to play out potential responses. Think about what it would be like if you responded from your cartoon world or from your real world.

**Cartoon World Responses**

- He "shouldn't" have said that.

- Scream at the person and demand that they "take back" what was said

- Other:

- 

- 

**Real World Responses**

- He did say that.

- Recognize what was actually said, and then have a non-threatening conversation around it

- Other:

- 

- 

You have said the wrong things at times in your life. What helped you change? Was it people screaming at you, laughing at you, mocking you, talking about you, demeaning you, putting you down --- all because they believed you "should" have said or done what they wanted....? Or was it you learning differently in some way? If you can recognize that being screamed at, belittled, demeaned, and put down doesn't work to help you want to change, then it's probably wise for you to understand the same is true for others when they say the wrong things. Change doesn't tend to occur when we demean others for not living how we think they "should," it occurs when our actions match our words and our lives become an example for others to follow.

Every time the word "**should**" comes to mind ("he/she shouldn't have said this or that," or "he/she should have done this or that…"), you are operating out of your *cartoon world*. Do your best to at least "catch yourself" using the word "should" or "shouldn't," and then, when you're ready, work to minimize or outright eliminate the use of that word.

**Applying What You Learn:**

1. Here is how the concept of Cartoon World / Real World directly applies to me:

_____

_____

_____

_____

2. Here is how I will look to use this concept today:

_____

_____

_____

_____

**Everyone has a cartoon world - that's completely natural; but only the entitled demand that others "should" live according to theirs.**

# "I Hardly Minimize at All"

**We have a tendency to minimize the hurt we cause others, but maximize the hurt others cause us.** We tend to downplay the things we say and do that are wrong, but we highlight or amplify the things that others say and do that's wrong. One of the most common ways that people can read others quickly is by listening for the way people minimize what they do. When we minimize the role we play, we don't take responsibility, and research has demonstrated overwhelmingly that people who do not take responsibly for the harm they cause and mistakes they make will continue to do what they do.

*"All I did* was raise my voice a little…."

"I *may* have said that…."

"I *wasn't trying* to…."

"I *didn't mean* to…"

"I *just* had to restrain her *a little*…"

## Real-life examples from three different individuals:

**Inmate:** "I'm not a drug dealer, I just had some pills and the other guy had some money, and I wanted the money and he wanted the pills, so we just made the exchange…."
**Counselor:** "That's the exact definition of a drug dealer."

**Inmate:** "They got me up in here for not making a truck payment." (Later, this same man admitted he got high on crystal meth and "hot-wired" a big rig truck… so technically, he didn't make a truck payment, but in reality, he minimized his stealing by reducing it to saying that "all he did was not make a payment…."

**Major**: "Is it true that you were caught red-handed with a metal shank?"
**Inmate**: "Well, not really. It was aluminum, and it just had some metal on the handle."

One of the most effective ways to break the habit of minimizing is to start by calling yourself out when you do it. To prepare yourself to be able to do this, let's start by taking events and purposely minimizing them the first time you describe them, and then state them next by taking complete responsibility. When we admit that we were wrong, we are not simultaneously saying that we are "always wrong" or that the other person didn't also play a role; instead, we are focusing on the only part over which we have control: ourselves and the actions we take.

In the following box, write down events from your past. In the left box, describe the situation in a way that purposefully minimizes your role, and then in the box on the right, describe the same situation, except this time accept complete responsibility for your part.

| MINIMIZING: | NOT MINIMIZING: |
| --- | --- |
| "I may have lashed out a little, but after what that CO said, how can you blame me?" | "I lost control and said some really inappropriate things to the CO. Regardless of what he said, I am responsible for me, and I was wrong." |
|  |  |
|  |  |
|  |  |

**Examples of minimizing words:**

- May / may have
- A little
- Maybe
- Didn't mean to
- Might /might have
- Didn't try to
- Kind of
- Yes, but…

The more you can openly talk about the way you have minimized in the past, the more growth others will see in you. The more you can show, with examples, ways that you now no longer minimize, the more likely others will be to see your changes. But if you continue to talk about "knowing" things and your actions are still the same old actions, then all you're doing is showing with your actions that you are actively trying to manipulate. Responsible human beings take complete responsibility for their actions. They fully own what they say and do, and they do not try to downplay the impact of their actions.

You have a choice, for instance, in working really hard to "beat the system," or in throwing yourself fully into trying to change. Here is an often hard-to-swallow fact: People who try to beat the system or get over on others are far less slick than they think. In other words, when people set out to "beat the system" or "get over" on others, that's much more obvious than the people who do it can see. So you are completely free to try to "beat the system," but it's worth it for you to understand that unless your actions match what you say, there is zero chance of you getting over on others. Unfortunately, all too often, when you are surrounded with others who also believe they can get over on others, you are much more likely to be convinced that you are "getting away" with something that you are not actually getting away with, because it's pretty obvious to others.

For example, people who work in prisons are not as naïve as inmates traditionally tend to think, and inmates are not as incapable as some staff traditionally tend to think. As with everything in life, there is always more to every situation than what people immediately think or readily see.

Push yourself to be the best version of yourself. The energy you spend on trying to get over on others would be best spent on actually just making the changes you need to make. The best way to make the changes you need to make is by accepting complete responsibility for everything you say and do. The more you can understand how easy it is for others to see when you minimize, the more effectively you can avoid minimizing altogether.

**Applying What You Learn:**

1. Here is how the concept of minimizing directly applies to me:

_____

_____

_____

_____

2. This is what others might see in my actions that would show them I am applying this concept to my life:

_____

_____

_____

_____

**The more accurate your language, the more responsibility you demonstrate.**

# THE IMPORTANCE OF MEANING MAKING

We are not defined by what happens to us in life, but by what we do with what happens to us in life. Whether we believe that we create our own meaning or meaning is bestowed on us from an outside source, the concept of "meaning" is one of the most incredible aspects to being human.

"He who has a why to live can bear almost any how."
- Friedrich Nietzsche

What is your meaning or purpose in life?

_____

_____

What do you do to show with your actions that your meaning actually guides your behavior?

_____

_____

In what ways do you allow other things to get in the way of your meaning?

_____

_____

In what ways does your meaning help you get through difficult moments in life?

_____

_____

If you're struggling to find meaning in your life, what steps will you take to pursue finding your meaning?

_____

_____

- Books you have or want to read about finding/creating meaning:

_____

_____

- People you can talk with that could help you discover your meaning:

_____

_____

- Self-reflection that you can do around meaning:

_____

_____

- Other:

_____

_____

## Recommended reading:

*Man's Search for Meaning*, by Viktor Frankl

Here are some options you can do around this recommended reading:

- You can choose to not even really look at this recommendation
- You can say that you "meant to look at it," and then fill in excuses for why you didn't
- You can assume that you already know everything that is in the book
- You can become defensive and say that no one can tell you what to do
- You can get the book, but never read it
- You can read parts of it
- You can get the book and just tell people that you've read it, even if you never read it
- You can read the book, sit with the ideas, but never apply them
- You can read the book and apply the ideas to your life
- You can read the book, apply the ideas to your life, and then talk to others about how you are trying to apply the ideas, including times when you are successful with it, and times when you are not successful with it – but you can continually focus on learning and growing as a person
- You can choose to say that all of this is "stupid," and keep doing what you've always done

All of these options (plus many more) are things that you can do. Each of these options has consequences. You are free to choose whatever you want to do, but you are responsible and accountable for whatever choice you make.

**Personal challenge:** Consider finding others who are willing to read the same books as you, and then challenge each other to really explore the concepts in those books with you.

This is my purpose in life:

_____

_____

_____

_____

_____

_____

**Applying Meaning: Writing a brief teaching tale about meaning**

Being able to step back and take a bigger view of any problem in front of you is a skill that can be developed. The faster you can take a larger view of any obstacle in front of you, the more options you will give yourself for getting beyond that obstacle.

Sometimes when we tell stories and use animals instead of people, we can create a teaching-tale that others can learn from (like the great Aesop did). **So for this exercise, challenge yourself to write a very brief story about an animal who finds his/her meaning or purpose, and then write a one-two sentence lesson out of it.**

For example, if I wanted to tell part of my own story around believing that my meaning is to help far more people than my own family, then I could write about a lion who learned that his greatest contribution to the world would be him learning to take care of far more than just his own family: This lion learned that his truest obligations in life are to all those he encounters. And I could put as many or as few details in my short story as I want.

**Once, there was a** _____

_____

_____

_____

_____

_____

_____

_____

_____

### *Why am I being asked to do this kind of exercise?*

The point of the exercise is to have you continually be clear with what your meaning is, and the more you talk about your meaning from creative parts of your brain, the more you are able to incorporate a well-rounded approach to learning. One great emotional management skill is the ability to see the same problem from as many viewpoints as possible, and the more you learn to tell your own story in the form of a parable (or short-teaching story), the easier it will be for you to see multiple perspectives faster (because when you write a story, you the author, are getting behind the eyes of all the characters you write about in your story).

**Self-evaluation:**

How can you apply the concept of meaning to helping you once you are free?

_____

_____

_____

_____

How will you (or won't you) apply this lesson to your life right now?

_____

_____

_____

_____

What behavioral examples can you site from your life that can show that you are actually applying this concept?

_____

_____

_____

_____

**When you find your true meaning, there are no limits to the lengths that you'll go to pursue it.**

# WHAT LED TO WHAT

"One thing has led to the next in the story of all of our lives."

What factors led to your current mental/physical incarceration?

- 
- 
- 
- 
- 
- 

From your perspective, describe why you are exactly where you are right now:

_____

_____

From the perspective of the authorities or outsiders, describe why you are exactly where you are right now:

_____

_____

From the perspective of your community, describe why you are exactly where you are right now:

_____

_____

From your family and friends' perspectives, describe why you are exactly where you are right now:

_____

_____

---

**It's everyone else's fault!**

You can blame everyone around you for why you are the way you are. There will never be a shortage of people and things to blame. The problem with blaming others, however, is that if everyone else really is to blame for your life, then you have to wait until they decide to let you be something different in order to change. But the reality is that it isn't everyone else's fault for why you are the way you are. You are the only person who has complete access to your mind. You are the only person in the world who can make your choices. The sooner you learn that, although you are not always responsible for what happens to you in life, you are always responsible for what you do with what happens to you in life.

The choice is yours. Change can start now.

Adapted from **The Anger Management Workbook**, by Dr. Christian Conte and Dr. Steve Miller.

---

# HOW AM I CHANGING?

People see our actions, not our intentions. In life, it never matters what we "meant to do" or "didn't mean to do," it only ever matters what we actually do. When it comes to personal growth, our actions speak much louder than our words. In this exercise, you are being invited to describe behavioral changes that you've made throughout the time you have spent incarcerated.

1. Describe a time in your life when your impulses got the best of you:

_____

_____

2. Describe how you are different now (for example, describe how your impulse control is more improved, and use an example to support what you describe):

_____

_____

3. Describe the types of issues in your past that would get to you the most:

_____

_____

4. Describe how you have changed, citing behavioral examples that demonstrate or support the changes you've made:

_____

_____

5.  If people described the "old you" from your past, how would they have described you?

_____

_____

6.  How might people who only met you recently describe you (In other words, what can people see in you by how you act and by what you talk about)?

_____

_____

If someone from your past comes up to you after not seeing him/her for years, there's a strong chance that your opinion of that person will at least immediately be influenced by what you knew of him/her in the past. Despite our natural desire for others to see the person we are now (not just who we were in the past), the reality is that in the same way that it is difficult for us to "just forget" what we know about others, the same is true about how others see us. That means if we really want others to see us differently, we have to show them with our actions.

7.  If people from your past interacted with you today, what changes would be obvious to them?

_____

_____

8.  In what ways do you still act, think, or speak like you did before you were incarcerated?

_____

_____

9. What is one of the most important things that you've learned about yourself that has been pivotal in helping you grow as a person – and, what is one of the most important things that you still want to learn about yourself?

_____

_____

10. Describe a person who you know who has not seemed to change or grow throughout the entire time you've known him/her (and names and details are not important here, the only thing that matters is being able to speak about the lack of changes you've seen) – And what advice might you give that person?

_____

_____

## Self-evaluation:

What are you taking away from doing this exercise?

_____

_____

_____

_____

How will you (or won't you) apply this lesson to your life right now?

_____

_____

_____

_____

What behavioral examples can you site from your life that can show that you are actually applying this concept?

_____

_____

_____

_____

**Answers in life are simple; accepting them is the real challenge.**

# TELL YOUR STORY

Many people never get a chance to tell their own story. In this exercise, you are being given an opportunity to tell your story. There are a few guidelines below to help you organize your story.

The elements of every story include:
- **Time period** (when the story takes place)

- **Setting** (place where story takes place)

- **Characters** (people in the story, including the main character, who, in your own story is you)

- **Theme** (action/adventure, mystery, tragedy, etc)

- **Plot** (storyline)

- **Conflict** (obstacles or challenges the main character faces; these obstacles could be within the main character's head, among many people, or any combination, etc)

- **Ending**

The short story you tell should include all of the elements of a story from above, but it can be as long as you would like to make it.

**Part I:** Tell your own story in a short-story format using the elements of a story above. Make sure you take your time and write out a complete short story of your life. Pick a theme to place your story in a context (the theme could be action/adventure, mystery, tragedy, etc.)

**Part II:** Tell your short story again, <u>except this time</u> tell your story from the context of a comedy, drama, action/adventure, etc. When you tell the story again, take your time and tell the story completely. The only difference will be in the way that you tell the story. Instead of telling the story in the context of fairness/unfairness or good/bad, tell the story in terms of comedy.

The goal of this exercise is to push yourself to tell your own life story from at least two entirely different perspectives, so it doesn't have to be just "short story" or "comedy," it can be any genre you would like. The point is to see your story from multiple angles. It will take a lot of time to complete this exercise in a way that makes it worthwhile, and it's important to allow yourself time to rewrite whatever you need to rewrite.

**Part I:**

_____

_____

_____

_____

_____

_____

_____

_____

_____

_____

_____

_____

_____

_____

**Part II:**

_____

_____

_____

_____

_____

_____

_____

_____

_____

_____

_____

_____

_____

_____

**Applying What You Learn:**

1. Here is how the concept of telling my story from multiple angles directly applies to me:

_____

_____

_____

_____

2. Here is how I have used this concept to grow today:

_____

_____

_____

_____

**You are the author of your life: Write wisely.**

# Self-Evaluation: Week One Review

One of the most important parts of personal growth is being able to give yourself honest feedback. There are no right or wrong answers here, there is only opportunity for awareness.

1.  On a scale of 1-10, rank where you see your personal growth right now.

1    2    3    4    5    6    7    8    9    10
Little growth                      Tremendous growth

Explanation:

_____

_____

2.  How aware are you of the way others view your actions:

1    2    3    4    5    6    7    8    9    10
Don't notice                      Very aware

Explanation:

_____

_____

3.  How aware are you of your own self-talk or inner dialogue:

1    2    3    4    5    6    7    8    9    10
Don't notice                      Very aware

Explanation:

_____

_____

4. How does looking at your own story from multiple perspectives impact you:

1    2    3    4    5    6    7    8    9    10

Don't notice                                           Very much

Explanation:

_____

_____

This is who I am right now:

_____

_____

_____

_____

This is who I am becoming:

_____

_____

_____

_____

These are the observable things that I am doing to become the best version of myself:

_____

_____

_____

This is how I would summarize my personal growth after this first week:

_____

_____

_____

This is my specific plan for approaching my next 7 days:

_____

_____

_____

**Pay attention to what you read, what you watch, and what you talk about, because whatever you put in your mind will be in your mind.**

# RESET

Older computers can be taken to experts to be wiped clean and reset. When this happens, the data and memory are cleared, but all the functions, abilities, and capabilities remain. It's a fresh start. Humans are far more complex than computers and cannot just be reset in the same way, but part of our complexity is that we have the ability to imagine very clearly what might happen if we were to be reset – and that is the goal of this exercise.

In this exercise, let's imagine that your mind is being wiped clean and reset. So starting tomorrow morning when you wake up, imagine that you woke up with the same intelligence, abilities, and capabilities, but you no longer operate from memory. Oh, and there is one major upgrade that happened in the reset: You now accept complete and total responsibility for everything you say and do, everything you think, and absolutely every bit of content that you contribute to the world.

Since this is a "reset" though, and nothing is damaged in your brain's internal hard drive, your mind will quickly fill back up with a constant inner dialogue, but now, since you don't have your old narrative playing in your head, you are completely free to create a new running internal dialogue. That is, you get to create from this moment forward, exactly what you want to focus on. You also get to reset what habits you engage in, what your new daily routine looks like, and what you choose to fill your mind with.

Imagine now that your mind was able to be reset, and that you now no longer had to play the same old narratives over and over in your head.

1. What would you choose to focus your thoughts on? (Remember, you would have no memory of past internal dialogue, so every single thought you have would be something that you are actively choosing to focus on having.)

_____

_____

2. What kinds of books would you read? (Think of things you want to learn, and think of the mind you want to build.)

_____

_____

3. What kinds of conversations would you have? (Again, it's important to remember for this exercise that you would not just be engaging in or repeating the old conversations that you usually have, because your memory for those would be gone. Remember that you now have complete freedom to only have conversations that are meaningful to you.)

_____

_____

4. What kinds of goals would you create? (Without a memory of what you "can't" do, you can build your new mind to be focused on creating clear goals that have you both identifying obstacles, as well as solutions for getting around those obstacles.)

_____

_____

5. What kinds of habits would you create for yourself? (Without a memory of negative self-talk or pessimism, you will be free to focus on creating and maintaining the kinds of habits that will help you achieve your goals.)

_____

_____

6. What kind of attitude would you create for yourself? (Without an ego that has to try to be 'right' and prove itself, you will now be free to create and cultivate literally any kind of attitude that would genuinely benefit your ultimate life goals.)

_____

_____

**At the end of our lives, in our final moments, we will all want peace, so it seems to make sense to me that we start striving for that peace now.**

After a complete mental 'reset,' how much energy do you think you would choose to put into the following:

| Behavior | Percentage of energy (%) |
|---|---|
| • Complaining | |
| • Expressing gratitude | |
| • Making excuses / justifying your actions | |
| • Blaming others | |
| • Meditating / Praying | |
| • Minimizing the harm you cause or mistakes you make | |
| • Finding peace | |
| • Gossiping | |
| • Convincing others that you're "right" about your beliefs | |
| • Working out | |
| • Reading | |
| • Watching TV | |
| • Challenging your own perspective | |
| • Trying to find ways to get others to do things for you | |
| • Helping others | |
| • Feeding your spirit | |
| • Learning about yourself | |
| • (Other): | |
| | |

## Self-evaluation:

What are you taking away from doing this exercise?

_____

_____

_____

How will you (or won't you) apply this lesson to your life right now?

_____

_____

_____

What behavioral examples can you site from your life that can show that you are actually applying this concept?

_____

_____

_____

**We are not always responsible for what happens to us in life, but we are always accountable for what we do with what happens to us in life. Every day is an incredible opportunity to reset, refocus, and work to give the world our absolute best.**

# ACTIONS SPEAK LOUDER THAN WORDS

If someone who hurt you in the past told you that he or she had changed, the first thing that you would want to see is how. You would look to see if the person's actions matched his or her words. The same is true for how others will view you. Regardless of what you say about how you have changed, the only thing others will key in on is whether or not your actions back up what you say. In this exercise, it's important to write out your daily schedule.

We master what we practice, and oftentimes we accrue bad habits because we don't realize that we're practicing them. To get an accurate understanding of the habits you have, write out your daily schedule, including why you do everything you do in a day. The more details you write now, the more you will have to compare against when you look at your growth by the end of this experience. You are not wrong for anything you write. The goal is twofold. First, to have you write down what you do so that you can see it in writing (which can help you acknowledge and own what you do) and second, to give you a baseline with which you can compare where you are at the end of this experience.

**DAILY**

MORNING:

_____

_____

AFTERNOON:

_____

_____

EVENING:

_____

_____

NIGHT:

_____

_____

When we stay locked in our own worldviews and our own perspectives, we often fail to see the impact of our actions on others. As long as you are in the world, you are going to interact with others, and knowing how to do so well is important. In this exercise, push yourself to try to see your actions from other people's perspectives.

1. Describe a situation where you had a hard time understanding why people reacted the way they did to you:

_____

_____

2. Upon reflection, from their perspective, here is what they likely saw in me by watching my actions:

_____

_____

3. Here is a situation I currently don't understand:

_____

_____

4. Here are possible explanations for the above situation from multiple perspectives:

_____

_____


**Applying What You Learn:**

1. Here is how the concept of actions-speak-louder-than-words directly applies to me:

_____

_____

_____

_____

2. Here is how I have used this concept today:

_____

_____

_____

_____


**Knowledge is meaningless without action.**

# Abusing Power

An inmate was angry at a guard who said something very unprofessional to him. The inmate said, "You are abusing your power! You're insecure in your own life, so you take it out on me. You're a joke!"

Then the inmate wanted to call his family. There was another, weaker inmate on the phone (and the man on the phone wasn't a part of the gang that ran the unit), so the angry inmate just kicked him off the phone. Then he called his family. He was angry about how the guard treated him (he was angry that the other weaker inmate dared to even use the phone without his permission), so he started screaming at his wife.

The angry inmate hated that the guard was insecure and abused his power - But he was so blinded by his own anger that he missed the fact that he acted in the *exact same way* toward those he had power over. He abused his power to the other inmate. He abused his power to his wife. But he only complained about the unfairness of the guard's power over him.

And because this is a true story, this man's response to being called out is worth knowing. When his counselor called him on his hypocrisy, this man shouted, "It doesn't matter what I do! Everyone else is the problem! And if you can't see that, you're the problem!" And then the other inmate who he abused his power over and kicked off the phone shrank back in fear. And his wife, after she hung up the phone from being yelled at and put down, she shrank back in fear, too. But the inmate who dominated both of them stayed angry, because he never cared about "people abusing power," he only ever cared if people abused power over him. He was absolutely fine with all those he dominated and abused, he just didn't want what he did to others to be done to him.

And it's not just him. The reality is that most people don't hate when others abuse power; they only hate when others abuse power over them. Most people are all-too-quick to use their own power and control over others, all the while complaining about others doing it to them.

The sad truth is that most people don't hate that others take things out on the wrong people, they only hate it when others take the wrong things out on them. And they certainly excuse themselves and rationalize and justify when they themselves take things out unnecessarily on others.

If you truly hate others abusing their power, and if you truly despise people taking things out on the wrong people - then start by changing the only person over whom you have control: Yourself.

**Ask yourself:**

- Over whom do you have power (or have had power over in the past)?

_____

_____

_____

- How did you treat those over whom you had power?

_____

_____

_____

- In what ways have you abused your own power?

_____

_____

_____

(If your first thought to how you treated others over whom you had power is that you treated them "fairly," then you are missing the point that you indeed had power over them, even though you might have seen yourself as a "benevolent ruler." This is an awakening fact, and often a tough pill to swallow. If your first thought was that you didn't have power over anyone, then you are practicing denial, as there are inherent power differences in human interactions. If your first thought was that you certainly have had power over others, and certainly have abused that power at times, then you are on a path to personal growth.)

- How have you displaced your anger onto others who didn't deserve it?

_____

_____

_____

_____

- In what ways have you downplayed or minimized your actions?

_____

_____

_____

_____

- Describe examples of how you have demanded in the past that others change their behaviors instead of you working on your own?

_____

_____

_____

_____

It's easy to sit back and demand that others not abuse their power. It's much more difficult to avoid abusing the power that you have. The insecure simply strive to overthrow others' power by putting themselves in power. The wise, the mature, and the compassionate instead learn about the inherent nature of power, and then they seek to demonstrate equality by their actions.

These are the ways that I have power over others:

_____

_____

_____

_____

These are the ways I can stop myself from hurting others when I have power over them:

_____

_____

_____

_____

## Applying What You Learn:

1. Here is how the concept of power directly applies to me:

_____

_____

_____

_____

2. Here is how I have applied this concept today:

_____

_____

_____

_____

**Power ebbs and flows. There are moments we have it and moments we don't. The more we focus on the way others don't use their power the way we think they "should," the less focus we have on the way we abuse our own power. Be mindful of how you are in moments where you have the upper-hand.**

# How EXTREME LANGUAGE Shapes Attitude

Pre-teen and teenage children frequently exaggerate by using extreme language to describe their world. They say things like, "Nobody listens to me!" and "Everybody's out to get me!" They use extreme words like:

- Always
- Never
- I can't stand it!
- Nothing

- Nobody
- Everybody
- It's not fair!
- Everything

The more that preteen and teenagers use extreme words to describe what's going on, the more extreme emotions they feel dash which is also a reason why they are so reactive and impulsive. Young people's brains are still developing, and the emotional center of the brain develops before the higher-level problem-solving center, so it makes sense why children use extreme adjectives to describe their world. The human brain isn't fully developed until a person's mid 20s, which explains why teenagers exaggerate and make mountains out of molehills. That's the way they see the world.

## The Difference that Accurate Language Makes

Because adults have fully-formed brains, it's easier for them to be rational and use accurate (instead of extreme) language. When adults use accurate language without exaggerating, they are more rational and reasonable. Adults who are stuck thinking like children, however, tend to continually use exaggerated language to describe their experiences. When you look at the difference between exaggerated, extreme language and accurate language, you can see each leads to very different kinds of reactions:

**Why we exaggerate:**

There are several reasons why we use exaggerated words as adults even though we understand logically that they are exacerbating the situation. The first reason is habit: We tend to do what we have always done. Remember, we master what we practice, even if we "didn't mean to" be practicing something.

The second reason we tend to exaggerate with our language is that when events trigger emotional responses in us, we tend to respond emotionally in kind. It's difficult to respond emotionally when we are logical and rational, so using extreme words allows us to have an excuse for why we are thinking the way that we are.

Take a look at the difference between using exaggerated, extreme words to describe an event, and using accurate, balanced language to describe the same situation.

| Extreme Words: | Accurate, Balanced Words: |
|---|---|
| "Nobody ever backs me up!" | "Two people disagreed with my perspective today." |
| "Everybody else gets whatever they want!" | "I didn't like seeing someone get something today that I didn't think he/she deserved." |
| "They always do this to us!" | "This is the third time this has happened to our group." |
| "I can't stand it when they do that!" | "I might not like it, but I can handle it." |
| "They get away with everything!" | "That person didn't get the consequences that I thought he/she *should* have gotten (but I realize my 'should' is an irrational cartoon world thought)." |

1. What differences do you notice between using exaggerated or extreme words and using accurate words?

_____

_____

2. What go-to extreme words do you tend to use the most?

_____

_____

3. Briefly describe a situation that angered you recently, but do so from two different perspectives. The first time, use exaggerated words to describe the event. The second time, use accurate, balanced adjectives to describe the same event.

    a. Exaggerated, extreme words:

_____

_____

_____

_____

    b. Using accurate, balanced words:

_____

_____

    c. What do you notice about how you feel as you reflect on the differences between the first time you described the event that angered you with extreme words and the second time when you described the same event with accurate, balanced language?

_____

_____

**Personal challenge: Make an effort to teach this lesson to someone today. The more you practice teaching this concept of accurate language versus exaggerated language, the better you get at doing it yourself.**

The goal is not to be perfect (which is just another extreme, anyway). The goal is to be aware of how the words you use impact the way you feel, and ultimately the choices you make. The more you learn to use accurate, truthful statements to describe what you experience, the less impulsive you will be.

**Extreme language examples:**

"No one here cares about any of us. Everyone here is so corrupt. The whole system is messed up. I never did anything!"

"I'm sick and tired of being the only one who…"

**Balanced language examples:**

"It's unfortunate things aren't happening the way I want right now, but it's not the end of the world, and I can handle it."

"I'm pretty frustrated right now, but I know every emotion has a beginning, middle and end, and I know this feeling will pass."

**Be mindful of what you say to yourself in your self-talk, because you are listening.**

# You Are Responsible for You

People don't always **do** what you want. People don't always **say** what you want. *Sometimes* people promise you things and, for whatever reason, end up not following through; other times people outright hurt you with what they say or do. The world does not always work out to your favor; BUT, *there are many times when it absolutely does*. **There are many times when things do go your way**. You are responsible for whether you choose to focus on the things that don't go your way or the things that do go your way.

You are NOT in control of what others say and do.

You are NOT always in control of the things that happen to you.

But no matter what others say or do, and no matter what happens to you in life, here are two facts that are essential to remember:

- **You are ALWAYS responsible for your actions.**

- **You are ALWAYS COMPLETELY responsible for how you handle whatever comes your way.**

Yes, things will be difficult. Yes, it can be tough at times to stay in control of your thoughts and actions, but, no matter what happens, even if it's difficult, you are strong enough and capable enough to get through any difficult situation. But even when you don't feel strong, even when you feel at your most vulnerable or most angry or most impulsive… in fact, no matter how you ever feel: You are responsible for you.

One of the most powerful concepts I have been grateful to share with the world is that *there is a beginning, middle and end to every emotional situation*. Regardless of any situation that comes up, remember that it will pass. Do your best to avoid making a poor decision in the beginning or middle of the situation that ultimately makes things worse for you down the road. Remember, too, that there is an enormous difference between what you *need* to have happen and what you *want* to have happen.

Emotions and impulses come and go, but actions last forever. Nothing you say can be unsaid. Nothing you do can be undone. Your anger is always understandable. You always have a right to feel however you feel; but you are also always accountable for whatever you do with those feelings.

**EXERCISE: Think about a possible situation** that you might experience that could potentially get to you in the future – and **then think of how you can handle it two ways**:

- If you were to let your impulses take over and handle the situation poorly, what would it look like (and what regrets would you ultimately have)?

_____

_____

_____

_____

- If you used your best self-control to handle the situation instead, what would it look like?

_____

_____

_____

_____

**Applying What You Learn:**

1. This is how I can apply this concept to my life right now:

2. Here is what others will notice about me as I continue to get better at applying this concept:

**The future will inevitably be here; do your best to make the kind of decisions now that your future self will appreciate.**

# Hypocritical

*"Son, you need to accept responsibility for your actions,"* says his father.

Later, that same father got in trouble at work. When he came home, he told his wife that it was his boss's fault for "spying on him," and that if his "boss wasn't watching, it wouldn't have been a big deal." The son overheard his father not take responsibility for his actions. The son then learned more by watching his father than by what his father told him. The father, of course, did not even realize his hypocrisy, which just gave him more confidence to tell others how to live, when he himself couldn't do what he asked of others.

*"I'm sick of people getting away with everything!"* complained the man.

Later, that very same man got caught doing something he wasn't supposed to do at work. He got several of his work buddies to go-to-bat for him, though, and defend him by badgering their supervisor, and then he didn't receive any discipline for what he did. He minimized what he did and just went on with his day. He even kept on preaching that other people get away with everything. He couldn't even see his hypocrisy.

*"People nowadays are so entitled! I can't stand it!"* complained the woman at work, and her colleagues all grumbled along in agreement with her.

Later on, that woman's manager asked her to do paperwork that she didn't feel like doing. She told her manager that she "shouldn't have to do the paperwork the way he wanted it done," because her way worked just fine for her. Then she gossiped about her manager, saying that she "shouldn't have to do things the way he wants them done." Her colleagues all agreed with her, and they all gossiped and made fun of the manager behind his back. None of them was insightful enough to see either their entitlement of their hypocrisy.

*"People need to be tolerant of others who are different from them!"* Shouted the young person at the political rally.

She then turned to a crowd of people supporting the other candidate and called them every negative name she could think of. She couldn't tolerate others for thinking differently from her, but she demanded that others show the kind of tolerance that she could not show.

*"Why can't the COs ever call each other on their mistakes? All they do is protect each other! That's not right! They should call each other out and turn each other in when they mess up!"* said the inmate, and he was furious.

Later that day, another inmate in that man's circle of friends did something really wrong, and when anyone questioned the inmate who was angry about the COs not calling each other on their mistakes, he simply denied knowing anything about it. He never challenged the other inmate, either, but he still went on to rally other inmates to be angry at COs for not calling each other out, even though there was no chance that he or any other inmates would turn each other in or even call each other out when they did things wrong. He couldn't even see his hypocrisy, and he certainly never changed what he did.

*"I hate participation trophies! They're such a joke! I would never allow my children to EVER accept a participation trophy, and I would never accept one myself!"* said the union member.

And then later that day, that union member cashed his check with the mandatory minimum raise in it. The "mandatory minimum raise" that he got for simply showing up to work. He did nothing to earn that raise except show up to get his "participation trophy," which he gladly accepted, and there was no way he would ever give that money up. Still, he couldn't see that he accepted a participation trophy every single time he got that yearly raise for simply showing up, and he couldn't face or accept his hypocrisy.

If these real-life examples of hypocrisy trigger you, then it's wise for you to stop focusing on others' hypocrisy, and instead focus on your own. The more you point out others' shortcomings, the less you focus on your own. Take time to reflect on your own hypocrisies, and then if you're willing, share them with others so that you can be held accountable for them in the future.

These next few questions can be some of the toughest to answer, but remember, no one said this would be easy. Push yourself to challenge your own perspectives. Push yourself to challenge your own ego, and do your best to answer these questions in the most honest way possible:

1. Describe some ways that you have acted hypocritically:

_____

_____

2. Describe specifically how you justified to yourself at that time that what you were doing either "wasn't" hypocritical, or perhaps you realized it by downplayed it.

_____

_____

3. Describe the potential ways you might act hypocritically in the future:

_____

_____

4. Describe how you intend to either catch yourself or outright stop yourself from acting in hypocritical ways moving forward:

_____

_____

**Others' hypocrisy angers us; our own hypocrisy blinds us: What we choose to focus on can either be the source of our rage or the source of our growth.**

# Personal Scouting Report

Professional athletes scout the opponents that they will compete against. The reason? The more they know about their opponents, the more prepared they are for the obstacles in front of them. Truly great athletes understand, too, that not only are they scouting their opponents, but also, their opponents are scouting them. If you know someone is scouting you, it's wise to have a sense of what they see.

In life, considering that every interaction you have with others requires you performing an action (i.e., communicating, etc.), then it is possible to evaluate your "performance" in life. Specifically, in this exercise, we will look at three primary areas that impact what you bring to the table every time you interact with others: Energy, Self-Talk, Communication.

Imagine that you are a professional scout and that your job is to assess talent. For this job, though, instead of doing a scouting report on a sport, you will be doing it on life; and instead of evaluating others, you will be scouting yourself. Now, of course your energy, self-talk and communication vary at different times, but there are overall patterns that we all tend to fall into. So evaluate yourself in terms of what you generally bring to the table in regard to *the energy you bring to a room*, *the kind of self-talk you have* (that gets reflected in they way you act), and *the actual communication you have with others* (your end of the communication or the part you play, only).

The more accurately you can assess your energy, self-talk and communication, the more accurately you will see how others experience you. Understanding how others experience us is essential for communicating clearly – which is a skill (clear communication with others) that can help you in every part of your life, beginning with getting work and thriving in a career path.

Take some time to complete the assessment tool on the following page.

***Self-Assessment:*** Rate yourself on the following chart, and then answer the questions below.

| | Positive | Neutral | Negative |
|---|---|---|---|
| | ‖‖‖‖‖‖‖‖‖‖‖‖‖‖‖‖‖‖‖‖‖‖‖‖‖‖ | ‖‖‖‖‖‖‖‖‖‖‖‖‖‖‖‖‖‖‖‖‖‖‖‖ | ‖‖‖‖‖‖‖‖‖‖‖‖‖‖‖‖‖‖‖‖‖‖‖‖‖‖ |
| **My Energy** | | | |
| **My Self-talk** | | | |
| **My Communication** | | | |

Typically, when I encounter negativity, I:

    **A.** Join in and contribute to it
    **B.** Shut down and don't say anything
    **C.** Redirect the conversation to make it solution-focused
    **D.** (Something else):_____

Given that **people only see my actions, not my intentions**: Here is what I believe people *see* when they interact with me: (Circle as many as apply)

    **A.** Someone who gossips
    **B.** A person who focuses on the negative more than the positive
    **C.** A disgruntled person
    **D.** A positive person
    **E.** A solution-focused person
    **F.** A complainer
    **G.** A leader
    **H.** A kind person
    **I.** An angry person
    **J.** A rigid person
    **K.** A flexible person
    **L.** Someone who says, *"Yes, but…"* a lot
    **M.** Someone who takes responsibility for my actions
    **N.** A person who takes myself too seriously
    **O.** A stressed out person
    **P.** A growing person
    **Q.** A peaceful person
    **R.** (Something else):_____

Some people's energy is draining to be around, other people's energy actually gives us energy. Some people's energy is anxious, some people's energy is calming. Energy levels change throughout the day, but in general, and *based on your self-scouting report:* **What kind of energy do you give off to others?**

_____

_____

_____

When people tell themselves constantly that things "aren't fair," or that nothing you ever give them is enough, because they always want more (but don't have the ability to see that they play the "yes, but" game, or that they are making excuses, so they believe their complaints are all "justified"). If you say to yourself that "Nobody ever gives you anything," that kind of statement will lead to very different energy than if you tell yourself that you are grateful for any and everything you do have. **Based on your self-scouting report, if you were to summarize where your self-talk is at this point in your personal growth development, how would you describe your self-talk?**

_____

_____

_____

People see our actions, not our intentions, and when it comes to communication, people only ever hear what we say, not what we don't say. **After doing a scouting report on your communication, how would you describe your communication at this point in your personal growth?**

_____

_____

_____

In regard to your scouting report on your energy, self-talk and communication, in what ways can you work on improving your energy?

_____

_____

_____

In what ways can you work on improving your self-talk?

_____

_____

_____

In what ways can you work on improving your communication?

_____

_____

_____

**You are worth your entire effort.**

# Taming the Dragon

A hermit who was a wildly talented artist lived in a cave by himself. This hermit was such an incredible artist that he painted a picture of a dragon on the back wall of a cave. The picture he created was so realistic looking, that one day, the picture he painted scared him so much that he ran out of the cave.

The people in the village below were bewildered at his actions. "Didn't he paint that picture himself?" they asked. "How is it that something of his own creation could scare him so much?"

But what the people didn't realize is that we are all like that talented hermit artist. We create stories in our minds that make us angry, and then we go with those stories, even though we are the ones who made those stories up in the first place.

We all have dragons to face. And many of the dragons we have to face are ones that we have created in our own minds.

The questions we all have to face are:

1.  What are the "dragons" in your own life?

_____

_____

2.  What led you to creating those dragons in your mind?

_____

_____

3.  How can you gain control of your mind to no longer be afraid of your dragons?

_____

_____

4. What peaceful images can you paint in your mind to replace the dragons that you've created?

_____

_____

People will never always act the way you want them to act or speak the way you want them to speak; however, you will always be responsible for how you respond to those people. The weak believe that others have painted the dragons they see in their minds, but the strong realize that each of us has painted own dragons, and each of us alone can defeat the dragons in our own minds.

What you fill your mind with will be in your mind. The music you listen to, the movies you watch, the books you read, the things you pay attention to, and the things you talk about all influence what gets "painted" in your mind. The more aware you are of where your "dragons" come from, the less afraid of them you'll be.

The power of visuals:
Draw your personal "dragon," and then draw an image of you taming your dragon.

**You are the only one with unrestricted access to your mind.**

# Self-Evaluation: Week Two Review

1. On a scale of 1-10, rank where you see your personal growth right now.

1    2    3    4    5    6    7    8    9    10
Little growth                                Tremendous growth

Explanation:

_____

_____

2. How aware are you of the way others view your actions:

1    2    3    4    5    6    7    8    9    10
Don't notice                                Very aware

Explanation:

_____

_____

3. How aware are you of your own self-talk or inner dialogue:

1    2    3    4    5    6    7    8    9    10
Don't notice                                Very aware

Explanation:

_____

_____

4. How would you rank the effort you put into your personal growth this week:

1   2   3   4   5   6   7   8   9   10
Not much                                Tremendous effort

Explanation:

_____

_____


Remember, this is all about you becoming the best version of yourself.
This is who I am right now:

_____

_____

_____

_____


This is who I am becoming:

_____

_____

_____

_____

These are the observable things that I am doing to become the best version of myself:

_____

_____

_____

This is how I would summarize what I've learned through this second week:

_____

_____

_____

This is my specific plan for approaching my next 7 days:

_____

_____

_____

**You are not your actions, but your actions alone define your legacy.**

# QUICK SHEET ON HOW TO STAY ANGRY

Sometimes it's easier to call ourselves on what we're doing ineffectively once we know exactly what doing the ineffective thing looks like. So in that spirit, here are 10 ways you can stay angry and miserable without ever having to challenge what you think or believe.

- **Assume the problem is others** – This is a great way to stay angry. The more you put the responsibility for how you feel on others, the less you have to do anything differently yourself.

    1. Give an example of a time when you assumed that the problem was other people and not your view of the situation:

    _____

    _____

- **Assume that others need to change in order for you to find peace** - which allows you to freely give them power over your life, and let's them control you like a puppet

    2. Give an example of a time when you convinced yourself that others needed to change in order for you to find peace:

    _____

    _____

- **Minimize your own faults, and amplify others' faults**

    3. Give an example of time when you downplayed your faults but highlighted or amplified others' faults:

    _____

    _____

- **Live in your cartoon world** – "This is how the world should be..."

    4. Give an example of a time when you lived in your cartoon world:

    _____

    _____


- **Fill your mind with the things you dislike** (Think of all the things that anger you, and then make sure you watch things, read things, and constantly talk about things that make you angry. This is a great key, by the way, to staying angry.)

    5. Give an example of a way in which you keep watching, reading, or talking about things that make you angry, when you have complete freedom to watch, read or talk about whatever you want:

    _____

    _____


- **Set out to actually change others** (Because you know it's impossible to change others, only yourself, this is a great way to keep yourself angry.)

    6. Give an example of a time when you tried to change others rather than change your perspective on others?

    _____

    _____

- **Rely on your biases to keep seeing the world the way you want to see it.**
  Hindsight bias (when you learn something new and then convince yourself that you "already knew it") and confirmation bias (when you look to see whatever you think you would see in others) both help you stay locked in anger, and what's more: if you ever lose steam for your anger and hatred, they can rekindle it for you)

  7. Give an example of a time when you used your biases to stay angry:

  _____

  _____

- **Use extreme language to describe your world (remember to use words like "Nobody ever…!" and "Everybody around here…" because the more extreme your words, the more extreme your anger.)**

  8. Give an example of some of the extreme words you tend to use that keep you locked in anger:

  _____

  _____

- **Be attached to what you think and believe**. (Even though you likely say that "as long as you're alive, you still have more to learn," one of the best ways to stay angry is to keep believing that you're right no matter what. The more attached you are to what you already know, the more limited you'll be to what you can know.)

  9. Give an example of something that you say you're open to challenging, but in actuality, you know you're not open to changing:

  _____

  _____

- **Play the yes-but game** - Say that all of this makes sense, then say "but" and go ahead and give yourself an excuse to keep living in misery.

    10. Give an example of a time when you played the yes-but game:

    _____

    _____

Now you have it: 10 ways to stay angry and miserable. If you willingly choose to do any or all of these 10 things, then you are consciously choosing to stay angry despite what you know. The more you know, the better decisions you can make.

Here is what stands out the most to me from this exercise:

_____

_____

_____

_____

_____

**If you knew a path led straight to the sewer, you would only take that path if you wanted to end up in the sewer; and if that's where you want to go, great, but if you don't want to end up there, then it's wise not to go that way.**

# Personal Growth Questions

Again, say to yourself: "**People see my actions, not my intentions.** It never matters what I "meant do" or "didn't mean to do," it only ever matters what I actually do. Knowing that is not enough: The key is to live it."

Here are powerful questions to ask yourself about what people learn about you by watching your behaviors:

- What do people learn about me by watching my behaviors?

_____

_____

- What am I teaching people about who I really am by my actions?

_____

_____

- Is my behavior an accurate reflection of my best self (if not, what can I do to make it so)?

_____

_____

- Would I act this way if I was out in public and the whole world was watching? In other words, is my behavior the same in front of the people I'm around now as it would be if I was around different people"

_____

_____

- Am I proud of where I am right now? (How so, or why not?)

_____

_____

_____

_____

- Here are ways in the past that I have downplayed my mistakes and then made a big effort to point out other people's mistakes?

_____

_____

- Are the behaviors I do a good reflection of who I want the world to see me as? (If not, what do I need to change most?)

_____

_____

- Here are ways that my actions have shown others that I am willing to be their puppet (even though I hate to admit it) and be reactive to what they say:

_____

_____

- How are my behaviors and perspective different from a teenagers' behaviors and perspectives?

_____

_____

- If my children were watching me, would I be proud of how I act?

(Would I be setting the kind of example that I want them to follow?)

_____

_____

- Do I play the "yes-but" game?

_____

_____

- Do I practice the kind of daily habits that help me improve every day? (If so, list them. If not, why not?)

_____

_____

_____

_____

If you are not proud of what you are showing people with your actions right now, then right now is the absolute best time to change those behaviors.

**No matter what others do, you will always be responsible for your own behaviors.**

# THE FIVE ERRORS OF COMMUNICATION

Over the years, I have found that there is a big difference between talking just to talk, and talking so that we can actually be heard. The hard truth is that sometimes our egos want to say something so badly that we don't care how we say something, but the fact is that it absolutely matters how we say anything we say.

We all make mistakes when we communicate. We're human, after all. When it comes to improving our communication, there's no better place to start than with ourselves. If you think about it, the one common factor in every communication you ever have is you. That is, you are a part of every communication you have. And since you already know that you are the only one you can control, it's smart to own your mistakes and then learn from them.

I developed what I call the Five Errors of Communication to help people understand the ways in which we shut others down from even listening to what we have to say.

In this exercise, imagine you are looking back on your old communications as if you are watching game film. The goal is to look at your old communications and try to figure out what you could have done more effectively, that way you'll know what you can do more effectively in your future communications. The goal is *not* to feel shame about making mistakes. The goal is simply to learn from them.

1. **ERROR OF APPROACH** – Occurs when we shut people down by the way we begin the conversation

- Happens when we're so intent on saying what we want to say that we fail to take the time it takes to communicate effectively
- The impulsive need to get our energy out is greater than our actual goal of communication
- Examples:
  - "Let me tell you why you're so stupid...."
  - "We need to talk...."

1. Give an example of a time when you shut others down from the first thing you said:

---

---

2.  Looking back on that interaction, how might you have approached that person differently so that you could have gotten through to them rather than shutting them down?

_____

_____

2. **ERROR OF INTERPRETATION** – Occurs when we fail to accurately understand what people are attempting to communicate with us

*   There is a difference between what people say (the content) and how they say it (the process).
    o   For example: "How are you?" She asked. "I'm fine!" He said, angrily.
    o   The error of interpretation occurs when we focus on the wrong part (i.e., either the content or process).
*   We know there is a difference at times between what we meant to say and how it actually came out, and the same thing occurs for others, but when we make the error of interpretation we fail to recognize that
*   Imagine blurring your eyes as you look at something: Stand back and get the whole picture without concerning yourself with the details.

3.  Describe a time when you misinterpreted what others have said in the past:

_____

_____

4.  Looking back on that interaction, what could you have done more effectively?

_____

_____

3. **ERROR OF JUDGMENT** – Occurs when we judge others rather than assess them

- Stereotypes: Our preconceived ideas of people get in the way of our communication
- Confirmation bias – When we look to see whatever we believe we'll see
- Examples:
    - o   "The gray shirts have no idea what it's like to have a hard life."
    - o   "All inmates are
    - o   "He's from _____, so that means he thinks _____."

5. Give an example of a time when you judged others:

_____

_____

6. Looking back now, how might have your communication gone differently if you avoided judging that person, and instead focused on simply assessing their behavior?

_____

_____

4. **ERROR OF LANGUAGE** – Occurs when we shut others down during the conversation
- The use of extreme language, such as "always," "never," "must," "have to," "can't," "should," "shouldn't," etc.
- Objectifying people (Difference between defining someone as a liar and saying they lied)
- Minimizing our own behaviors while maximizing others' behaviors

7. Give an example of a time when you made the error of language:

_____

_____

8. What accurate, balanced words could you have used instead, and, what impact might those words have had on you or others?

_____

_____


5. **ERROR OF OMNIPOTENCE** – Occurs when we accept responsibility for other people's actions
   - Taking anything personally that someone else does (e.g., someone taking or not taking your advice, etc.)
   - Example: Parents taking their children's actions personally (or defending them blindly without taking into account their actions

9. Give an example of a time when you felt responsible for others' actions:

_____

_____


10. Give an example of what you can do moving forward to avoid making this error?

_____

_____


It's important to consistently evaluate the ways in which you make the Errors of Communication so that you can accurately recognize why your communication is not as effective as you want it to be. *Make your language as accurate as possible*.

The more you take an honest look at your communication skills, the better you get at communicating. Communication, like everything else in life, takes practice. It's frustrating when others misunderstand us, and we can only put the blame on "everybody else" for so long before we have to come to terms with the fact that we play an equally big role in our interactions with others as well.

We all know that it's foolish to do the same thing over and over again and expect a different result. Just the same, it's also equally foolish to think that we all don't make mistakes communicating. We're human, and we all make mistakes. An inability to identify what you do ineffectively means you are likely to keep repeating the same mistakes; so this exercise is intended to help you identify exactly what you do ineffectively when you communicate so that you don't keep making the same mistakes over and over again.

**Applying What You Learn:**

1. Here is how the errors of communication directly apply to me:

_____

_____

_____

_____

2. Here is how I have specifically used this concept today:

_____

_____

_____

_____

*Identify the mistakes you make when you communicate with others, or you will be doomed to keep making those same mistakes.*

# What You Contribute to the World

When it comes to a movie, everything you see and hear - all the people in the movie, and everything they say and do comprises the "content" of the movie. Likewise, in life, everything each of us says and does comprises the "content" of the universe. **Every single thing that you say and do in your life constitutes your contribution to the world.** So, when you *say* something out loud, you are contributing content to the world; when you *do* something, that too, is your content. Every day the world resets with an entirely new "blank canvas," and every single thing you say and do will become a part of what you are actually contributing to the world that day.

You can think of the universe like a book or movie that's being written, and every single day, every word you say and every action you take is absolutely included in that book or movie. The question this exercise is asking you to think about is this: What is it that you are contributing to this world?

In other words, if you find yourself stuck in a cycle of complaining and blaming others for things in your life, then you are contributing complaining and blaming to the world. If you are constantly working to help others or improve the world in some way, then you are contributing kindness and helpfulness to the world. Whatever you say, whatever you do, remember, it never matters what you "meant to say or do" or "didn't mean to say or do," it only ever matters what you actually say or do.

Imagine that this following blank canvas represents what you contributed to the world today based on everything you said and did. Draw what you believe your contribution to the world was today. Remember, this is not about looking at only the good things you did or negative things you did. Instead, this is about taking a very hard look at ALL of the content you contributed to the world today. If the content you contributed to the world today was a drawing/painting/picture, what would it look like?

**TODLY:**

Every "today" is followed by a "tomorrow," so now let's look at what impact you can have tomorrow.

Now that you've drawn a picture based on what content you gave the world today, picture yourself completely resetting for tomorrow. In other words, tomorrow you can wake up with the complete understanding that everything you say and do, no matter how small, will impact the world in some way. On the following canvas, draw the kind of impact that you will strive to have tomorrow.

**TOMORROW:**

Think about the impact you hope to have on the world from this moment forward. Do your best to try to set your ego aside and objectively look at your impact from an outside perspective. The more clear you are with the meaning you want your life to have, the more you can create thoughts, words and actions that can support you having the kind of impact that you hope to have.

As long as you're alive, your words and actions will impact others. Adding content to the world is inescapable, but it is optional when it comes to what kind of content you give the world – and that is entirely up to you. We are all leaving a legacy no matter what we do in life; but what we contribute in life is the defining piece to what our legacies actually become.

1.  If the entire legacy you leave the world begins with ONLY what you do from this moment forward for the rest of your life, what would you like that legacy to be?

_____

_____

_____

_____

_____

_____

_____

_____

_____

_____

**You are the only one who is leaving your legacy.**

# Confusing Your Mind for Growth

When it comes to working out, there is a very simple guideline that states if you do the same number of reps and sets with the same weight, eventually you will hit a plateau or "stuck point." If you want to build muscle or just get the most out of your workouts, it's really important to "confuse" your muscles by doing different exercises, different reps and different sets. When you mix things up and when your muscles don't know what to expect, growth happens.

The same is true of your mind.

*If you talk about the same things you always talk about and do the same things you've always done, you will continue to know what you've always known and get the same results you've always gotten.* If you want to grow mentally, it's important to change up what you learn and the way you see the world. So right now, in this exercise, it's time to change up your conversations and change up what you do.

**Exercise 1:**
Start with the assumption that you are wrong about what you think and believe, and that what you know is not complete information. Next, engage others in conversations where you see them as experts whom you really want to learn from. Engage in conversations from this perspective, and then go back and journal about your experiences.

***Things to consider:***

- Did your ego allow you to be humble enough to stay in the position of constant learner, or did you find yourself jumping in to tell others how what they think/feel/believe is "wrong"?


- What did you learn by listening without trying to convince or convert others to think the way you do?

**Exercise 2:**

Speak from a place of radial responsibility. In other words, have conversations with others where you place complete responsibility on yourself. Operate, for this exercise, on the assumption that your influence on others caused them to think, feel, say or do whatever they did. With that, also assume complete ownership of anything negative that happens. For this exercise, do not justify, minimize or downplay the role you had, but instead, play up the role that you had, even the role you had in any negative outcomes. This is just an exercise, but the goal is to shake up the way you experience conversations and interactions.

*Example:*
"I was the one who let my fear and insecurities get the best of me. I know people see my actions, not my intentions, so it doesn't matter what my intentions were, at the end of the day, the reality is that I did do what they said. I was 100% wrong. What I learned about myself is that I can sit with uncomfortable feelings without feeling like I have to act on them. So that's what I'll do moving forward."

Your example:

_____

_____

_____

_____

*Things to consider:*

* *Think about the ways that you find yourself justifying or downplaying what happened.*
* *Think about the words you use to describe what you did. Words like, "All I did was…" or "I only…" or "I just…" mean you are downplaying the role you had.*

**Applying What You Learn:**

1.  Here is how the concept of shaking up what I always think and do directly applies to me:

_____

_____


**TO BE ANSWERED AT THE END OF THE DAY:**

2.  Here is how I have applied this concept today:

_____

_____


*Keep your mind on its toes.*

# Self-Counseling

The best counselor you can ever see is you. You are the only one in the world with complete, unfiltered access to your internal world. You are the only one in the world who can actually change your thoughts around. You are definitely the only one who can control your behaviors. In this exercise, let's look at what a counseling session would look like *if you were your counselor*.

**You the counselor:** So what are you struggling with *right now*?

**You, client:** (Answer)

_____

_____

**You, the counselor:** So what have you been *doing* to try to get through that?

**You, the client:** (Answer)

_____

_____

**You, the counselor:** *Is what you're doing working*?

**You, the client:** (Answer)

_____

_____

**You, the counselor:** If what you're doing honestly isn't working, then what do you think you can do differently? And don't tell me "nothing," because, remember, I am you! So I know that you know there are other things you can try. So what do you think they are?

**You, the client:** (Answer)

_____

_____

**You, the counselor:** *You are way more capable of solving your struggles than you give yourself credit for being. I'm confident in you. Keep working. Keep searching your mind for solutions. The path to peace isn't always easy, but it is possible.*

**Applying What You Learn:**

1. Here is how I can apply the concept of self-counseling to either a current problem I have or the next genuine problem I encounter:

*"I am the master of my fate: I am the captain of my soul."*

*- William Ernest Henley (from his poem, Invictus)*

# Seeing Many Sides

Think of a box. Boxes have four sides, plus a bottom, and a top, as well as an inside perspective and an outside perspective. Like a box, every single situation in life has multiple ways to look at it. The more emotional we are or the more narrow-minded we are the fewer sides to a situation we can see. The more rational we are or the more open minded or intelligent we are, the more sides we can see. The more we ask others for help seeing, the more sides we can see, but ultimately, none of us (not even combined) is all-knowing; therefore, there will always be sides or angles or factors to situations that we simply cannot see.

The more we are able to consider as many sides to every situation as possible the more aware we become that the smartest people see the most perspectives, and the wisest people recognize that it is impossible to see all the perspectives.

The more you realize that seeing all perspectives is impossible, the easier it is to let go of that feeling of certainty that you're "right," and anyone who disagrees with you is wrong. Ultimately the more you realize that you only ever see one or two sides of a box, the more you become genuinely humble

Think of a current (or the most recent) situation that bothered or angered you. Then write down at least 5 different perspectives to that same situation.

Briefly describe the situation:

_____

_____

_____

1.  Perspective #1

_____

_____

2.  Perspective #2

_____

_____

3.  Perspective #3

_____

_____

4.  Perspective #4

_____

_____

5.  Perspective #5

_____

_____

**Applying What You Learn:**

1. Here is how the concept of seeing things from multiple perspectives directly applies to me:

_____

_____

_____

_____

2. Here is how I can absolutely use this concept starting right now:

_____

_____

_____

_____

*Be mindful that the more you think you know, the less you actually understand.*

# How Change Happens

If you were invited to a party that you really wanted to attend, there would be two basic, but essential questions that you would have to find answers to before you could go:

1. Where is it?

2. How will you get there?

If you don't know where it is, you cannot get there. If you don't have a way to get there, you cannot get there. It's that simple.

The same is true about people changing. If a person tells you, "You need to be different!" but doesn't tell you *what* needs to change or what specifically you can work on to be different, then how can you possibly be expected to make any changes?

Change in any area of life is like this, too. Both for others and for you. The more you want actual change to happen in your life, the more specific you have to be about what it is that you want to change.

Now, maybe people will take your suggestions, and maybe they won't, but there is a 0% chance that anyone will take any of your suggestions if you don't actually make any. That is why this is a very important exercise.

This is an intellectual exercise, not an emotional one. For example, if you are emotional, you might say things like, "It doesn't matter what I say, nothing will ever change!" or "Nobody's gonna listen to me!" or "People never listen to me," or some other statement using extreme words like, "nobody" or "everybody" or "always" or "never," or maybe even some other exaggerated adjectives that aren't accurate.

We all need time to just be emotional and be angry or hurt that the world isn't the way we think it should be (and that's fine if that's where you are right now); but being emotional constantly without taking a break to be analytical and try to find real solutions is more reflective of what teenagers tend to do, not adults – so once you've given yourself enough time to be emotional, come back to this exercise and try it from a place of reason.

1. What would you like to see be different in the world?

_____

_____

2. How would you suggest that change happens?

_____

_____

3. What would you like to see differently in this 21-day program? In other words, how "should" this program be designed to help you learn about yourself?

_____

_____

4. How would you suggest that change happens?

_____

_____

5. What would you like to see be different about your own thoughts and actions?

_____

_____

6. How would you suggest that change happens?

_____

_____

It's easy to declare that others "should change." It's easy to sit back and say that things "should be different." But it's another thing altogether to put together a detailed, realistic plan to make those changes. When we talk from our cartoon worlds, we demand that others should think, feel, believe and behave the way we want; but when we operate from the real world, we are able to align our expectations with reality and make clear, achievable goals, both for ourselves and others.

Weak-minded people spend a lot of time criticizing others and demanding that they change. Weak-minded people like to sit back and demand that others do what they themselves are not willing to do. For example, a person who is out-of-shape has very little credibility to tell others what they "should" do to be in shape. A poor person has very little credibility for telling others how to accumulate wealth. A lazy person has very little credibility demanding that others work hard. So when out-of-shape people demean others for being out of shape, or when poor people mock others for not being able to have wealth, or when lazy people get angry with others for not working hard, all of that is easily categorized as "weak-minded."

There is, of course, an enormous difference between giving others feedback and criticizing them; but weak-minded people are usually unable to understand that difference. Feedback is intended to help others grow; criticism is intended to put others down. Feedback is constructive and centers on tangible concepts regarding what others can work on; criticism centers on demeaning others.

A great "rule of thumb" when it comes to giving feedback is that if you don't have the courage to live your message, then it's wise not to tell others that they "should" be doing what you yourself are either unwilling or unable to do. Critics lack the courage to do things themselves, so they operate out of their Cartoon World. Those who give feedback, however, operate out of the Real World; that is, they think in terms of problem-solving. Critics, on the other hand, think only in terms of complaining. Theodore Roosevelt spoke a famous quote about critics.

# The Critic

*"It is not the critic who counts; not the man who points out how the strong man stumbles, or where the doer of deeds could have done them better. The credit belongs to the man who is actually in the arena, whose face is marred by dust and sweat and blood; who strives valiantly; who errs, who comes short again and again, because there is no effort without error and shortcoming; but who does actually strive to do the deeds; who knows great enthusiasms, the great devotions; who spends himself in a worthy cause; who at the best knows in the end the triumph of high achievement, and who at the worst, if he fails, at least fails while daring greatly, so that his place shall never be with those cold and timid souls who neither know victory nor defeat."*

- Theodore Roosevelt

This saying is a powerful statement when used by those who have the courage to try in life. When this saying is referred to by weak-minded people who are stuck in the victim role, however, it rings hollow. For example, insecure and fearful people will often use this statement to declare: "Don't criticize me!" But what they are really saying is: "Don't give me feedback!" But that is not what Theodore Roosevelt meant by this at all.

The purpose of this statement was to resoundingly proclaim to those who are not in the arena: "Don't criticize me unless you're willing to be in the arena with me!" And that is vastly different than saying, "Don't ever criticize anything I do…." **Those who have the courage to live are also open to feedback** that helps them learn and grow. And those who are unwilling to throw themselves out there in the first place, as well as those who are unwilling to live their own message, would do well to silence their hollow criticism.

Do what you can to actively seek feedback. But more than that: Make sure that your reaction to the feedback you get shows people with your actions that you are actually open to feedback. In other words, if you ask for feedback and then get defensive when others tell you what they see, then they will be much less likely to give you honest feedback in the future.

Be mindful to give others feedback en route to their own changes; be mindful to be open to feedback when others offer it to you.

**Challenge yourself to challenge yourself.**

# Understanding the Victim Mentality:
## How Playing the Role of a Helpless Victim is Negative and Toxic

There is a fundamental difference *between someone who is victimized* and *someone who "plays the victim."* To be victimized is to be harmed, injured or killed as the result of a crime, accident, or other event or action. To "play the victim" is to minimize the role you play in interactions, to avoid accepting responsibility for your words and actions, and to put the onus for your life on others. To be victimized is to be violated, and the result can be traumatic. On the other hand, to play the victim, however, is to violate others by inaccurately blaming them for your own words and actions.

On an individual level, perhaps the biggest obstacle that playing the victim creates is an unwarranted sense of helplessness. People who have adopted a victim mentality convince themselves that they are not responsible for the role they play in interactions and systems, and they regularly practice avoiding responsibility by doing things like practicing minimizing the pain they cause others and the mistakes they make, but amplifying the pain that others cause them or the mistakes that others make.

On a systems level, perhaps the biggest obstacle that playing the victim creates is toxic negativity. Because people who play the victim tend to operate with a sense of entitlement, they see their negativity as justified and acceptable, and therefore have limited awareness of the negative impact they have on others. People who utilize the victim mentality convince themselves that others "should" think, feel, believe and behave according to their own self-centered narrative, and they often struggle to understand how others can see things differently.

People who operate with a victim mentality often speak in extremes. For example, they might say things along the lines of, "Nobody" or "everybody" or "never" or "always" to describe situations that do not, in fact, accurately encompass the range described. The more intensely we describe a situation as extreme, the more permission we give ourselves to respond accordingly. Therefore, people who play the victim role often make situations more emotionally charged than they need to be, and then blame others for why they do what they do. People who rely on extreme descriptions usually do so to either avoid accepting responsibility for their actions, or to rally others to share in their unrest or emotional upheaval.
Adopting the victim mentality inhibits people from striving to change, because they tend to focus on what others "should" or "shouldn't" do, and  emphasize their powerlessness.

The goal, then, is to move away from a victim mentality and instead adopt a healthy mentality, and the fastest route to a healthy mentality begins with accurate, balanced language, and with accepting complete responsibility for what we say and do. So what can we do?

The fastest path out of "playing the victim" is to own the reality that you are responsible for everything you say, do, think and feel. The more you own complete responsibility for your words and actions, and the less you downplay or minimize the harm you cause, mistakes you make, and negative impact you have on others, the sooner you will put the onus of change on yourself, and the faster you will move away from the victim mentality.

Here are some practical ways to move from the victim mentality to an empowered, healthy mentality:

| People with a Victim Mentality: | People with a Healthy Mentality: |
| --- | --- |
| • Minimize the role they play in interactions | • Accept complete responsibility for the role they play in interactions |
| • Tend to use inaccurately extreme adjectives to describe their experiences | • Tend to use accurate, balanced language to describe their experiences |
| • Focus on and complain about things that cannot change, such as the past | • Actively seek solutions for what can be done in the present moment |
| • Focus on what they believe "should" have happened and focus on what others "should" do differently | • Focus on accurately assessing the situation that actually exists, and on what they themselves can do from this moment forward |
| • View others' problems and challenges as simple, but view their own as complicated | • Recognize that others also face unseen and unidentified challenges |
| • Focus on who they can blame for their own actions and what cannot be done (i.e., helplessness) | • Focus on what they can learn from every interaction, and on how they can constantly improve |
| • Deny, minimize, or outright fail to see how their negative and toxic behavior impacts those around them | • Have an accurate perception of how their attitude, energy and communication style impacts others |
| • Tend to believe that they have the right answers, which makes them less open to feedback or attempting to see themselves the way others see them | • Recognize that their perspective is inherently limited, that they can learn and grow from every interaction, and that others see their actions, not their intentions |

# How to Empower Yourself Out of Victim Mode:

1. One thing that I am passionate about is:

   _____

   _____

2. What I want people to see about this issue is:

   _____

   _____

3. The value in taking the opposite perspective from my own is:

   _____

   _____

4. Something that angers me is:

   _____

   _____

5. What I *need* people to understand about that is:

   _____

   _____

6. What I *would like* people to understand about that subject is:

   _____

   _____

7. The difference between what I *need* people to understand about that topic and what *I want* people to understand about that topic is:

_____

_____

8. What I can personally do about the topic that angers me is:

_____

_____

9. The role I play in the story of this issue is:

_____

_____

10. The only person I can control is _____. The way I can change my behavior or alter the way I speak to those who see things differently to potentially impact them is:

_____

_____

*The more you practice not taking others' differences of opinion personally, the better you get at not taking others' perspectives personally.*

# Types of Anger

Everyone experiences anger. Anger is a natural emotion, and quite frankly, usually we have some pretty good reasons to be angry. Sometimes anger really is about anger, but a lot of times; most of the time, actually, anger is about something more. In fact, that is why I have seen people through the years initially be resistant to my anger management books and classes and programs - that is, until they quickly learn that anger management is really "emotional management," and it's about how we handle all of our intense experiences, including fear, anxiety, depression and trauma.

One of the great anger management experts in the world is Dr. Ron Potter-Efron, and he broke down different "types" of rage that we can experience. Think of "rage" on a continuum of anger. Whereas "mildly frustrating" might be on one end of that continuum, on the other end is rage. Whether you would call what you're experiencing "rage" or just "anger," understanding the following five types of rage are an important part of gaining maximum self-control.

Here are the types of rage:

**Sudden rage** comes on quickly and makes you feel out of control. **Seething rage** occurs when we allow our thoughts to make a situation get bigger after we walk away from it, because we can't stop thinking about it (so basically we make it bigger and bigger in our minds after we walk away). **Impotent rage** happens when we feel powerless about a situation. **Abandonment rage** happens when we feel like we're going to be abandoned. **Shame-based rage** occurs when we feel bad about who we are.

At the end of the day, no matter why we feel the anger we feel (which is certainly justifiable), we are ultimately responsible for anything we do no matter how we feel. The more you understand why you feel the way you do, however, the better chance you have at handling that feeling when it arises.

The good news is that there is an "antidote" to all of these types of rage. In the following exercise, do your best to write down the clearest examples possible. For the second part of each example, you'll be asked to push yourself to figure out the best possible realistic solution that you can.

**Sudden Rage – Comes on quickly and feels out of your control**

- Describe an example of a time when you experienced sudden rage:

_____

_____

_____

**Antidote to sudden rage:** Because sudden rage comes on so quickly and is rooted in you feeling threatened, the antidote to sudden rage is quickly reassuring yourself that you are safe in this particular situation. Specifically, saying things to yourself like, "I'm okay," or "I'm safe," or "It's cool," (or use whatever words fit for you to tell yourself that you are currently safe).

- What type of words of phrase would be realistic for you to use to help you get through sudden rage in the future?

_____

_____

_____

**Seething Rage – When we allow our thoughts to grow a situation once we walk away from it**

- Describe an example of a time when you experienced seething rage:

_____

_____

_____

**Antidote to seething rage:** Because seething rage is grounded in allowing your mind to spiral downward, making things worse and worse in your head, it is very important to tell yourself accurate, balanced language about the reality of the situation. The antidote involves avoiding any extreme words, such as "never," "always," "forever," "hopeless," etc.

• What types of words or phrases can you use to help you get through seething rage in the future?

_____

_____

_____

**Impotent Rage** – Occurs when we feel helpless to do anything about a situation (We tend to overcompensate by going from the feeling of powerlessness to the feeling of wanting to be in complete control of the situation)

• Give an example of a time when you felt impotent rage (something that's pretty common in prison, given the fact that you have so little control over so many different areas of your life in prison).

_____

_____

_____

**The antidote to impotent rage** is to focus on whatever it is that you can control. That is, you can control your self-talk, your actions, and the meaning you make out of every given situation.

• What types of words or phrases can you say to yourself the next time you feel impotent rage that can realistically help you get through impotent rage in the future?

_____

_____

_____

**Abandonment Rage** – Occurs when we perceive that we are going to be left or abandoned (even if it's only a perception of being abandoned, and not actually based on reality)

• Give an example of a time when you experienced abandonment rage.

_____

_____

_____

**The antidote to abandonment rage** is to talk to yourself in accurate, truthful ways about what abandonment really means. For example, if you were abandoned by your group 10,000 years ago in the wilderness of the earth at that time, being abandoned might have meant complete aloneness and certain death. In our current times, if your relationship partner leaves the relationship, you might feel "abandoned," but the reality is that you only lost a relationship, you did not lose your connection to humanity or your only means of survival. Therefore the antidote to abandonment rage is to be truthful to yourself about what really happened (i.e., "I really love this person and she no longer wants to be in a relationship with me, and even though this hurts very much, it's not the end of the world, and I can handle it.").

• What types of words or phrases can you tell yourself the next time you experience any sense of abandonment that can help you get through the emotion of anger?

_____

_____

_____

**Shame-based Rage** – Occurs when we feel we've been disrespected or feel shame

• Give an example of a time when you experienced shame-based rage.

_____

_____

_____

**The antidote to shame-based rage** is to clearly understand the difference between shame and guilt. Guilt is feeling bad about something you have done. Guilt is healthy, and if you feel bad about something you have done, that can be a good thing. The goal then, is to recognize the hurt you have caused, learn from it, and never do it again. Shame, on the other hand, is feeling bad, not about **what** you've done, but about **who you are**. And shame leads to more shame, more acting out, and more hurting others - or what I call a "cycle of shame." The antidote to shame-based rage is to acknowledge that you are not your mistakes, to learn from them, and to move forward being better from what you learned.

- What types of things can you say to yourself that might help you the next time you experience shame-based rage?

_____

_____

_____

**Applying What You Learn:**

1.  Here is the type of rage that I seem to have relied on the most throughout my life:

    _____

    _____

    _____

2.  Here is what I will do from this moment forward around anger:

    _____

    _____

    _____

*Awareness is essential to change but it's not enough: For real change to occur in your life, you must take action.*

# Self-Evaluation: Personal Development

Here is how I would rank my overall progress of my personal development as of right now:

- These are my strengths right now:

_____

_____

- This is what I have been learning about myself recently:

_____

_____

- These are areas where I still need to improve:

_____

_____

- This is what I am actively doing to work on those areas:

_____

_____

- These are the outside factors that impact me the most:

_____

_____

- This is what I am doing to become more effective at handling those outside factors:

_____

_____

- This is what others have noticed about me recently:

_____

_____

- This is what I still get defensive about:

_____

_____

- This is what I wish others saw about my effort (although I realize that others see my actions, not my intentions):

_____

_____

*The deeper into your mind you travel, the more you learn.*

# Stages of Change

| Precontemplation<br>x | Contemplation | Preparation | Action<br>O |
|---|---|---|---|
| Not even thinking about change | Thinking about change, but not ready to do anything about it yet | Making small changes | Completely changing |

Before we make any kind of changes in our lives, we go through a series of stages. Drs. Prochatska and DiClimente developed a model of how change happens. They call it the "stages of change." When we look at change through the stages of change model, we see that there are very specific stages that we go through. Now, the reality is that sometimes we can go through these stages in minutes, and sometimes they take many years. There is no "right way" to go through them.

When it comes to helping other people move through the stages of change, if we try to force them to be where they're not, we only end up with them being resistant.

Remember, it's easier for us to talk about the changes others "should" make than it is for them to make those changes. I created something called Yield Theory to help people connect with others and motivate them to make changes without making them defensive. In short, it's about meeting people where they actually are and not being the "fool on the mountain."

In other words, sometimes people are at "X," but we really want them to be at "O." When that happens, we tend to talk **at** others, or *nag* them. It's important to understand that, just as you're not always ready to make all the changes that might be good for you, others are also not always ready to make the changes you would like them to make. If you really want to help others change, it's important to take the time to meet them where they actually are, rather than try to talk to them as though they are somewhere where they just simply aren't. Yield Theory is about taking the time to meet people where they are in *every* conversation that you have with them.

- Give an example of a time when you weren't even thinking about changing something, but others in your life kept wanting you to change something.

---

---

- Give an example of a time in your life when you were thinking about change, but weren't quite ready to actually start working on that change yet.

  _____

  _____

- Give an example of a time in your life when you were making small changes toward your goal, but weren't quite all the way in making the change yet.

  _____

  _____

- Give an example of something that you set out to change, and actually followed through with completely changing.

  _____

  _____

| Precontemplation | Contemplation | Preparation | Action |
|---|---|---|---|
| x | | | O |

```
|_____|_____|_____|_____|
```

| Not even thinking about change | Thinking about change, but not ready to do anything about it yet | Making small changes | Completely changing |

Think about the Stages of Change in terms of *how you communicate with others*.

5. Give an example of a time when someone you were talking to was in the precontemplation stage of change, but you talked to her/him as though she/he *should* have been in the action stage.

_____

_____

6. Give a specific example of how you might be able to use this information to better meet people where they are in an upcoming conversation or interaction.

_____

_____

**Applying What You Learn:**

1.  Here is how the concept of the stages of change directly applies to me:

_____

_____

_____

_____

2.  Here is how I have used this concept today:

_____

_____

_____

_____

*Only fools demand that a man magically be where he isn't.*

# Driving Up the Mountain

A man set out to drive to the top of the mountain. He had set out on this very same trip many times in the past, and each trip resulted in the same outcome: His car broke down and his trip could not continue. Now, he really, really wants to drive up this mountain, and he only has one car.

This man is really anxious to get going on his journey, and there is no one telling him that he has to check his car before he leaves, but the history of his car breaking down every single time is a fact.

Here's the clincher: This man is physically stuck in a place where he has:

- Time to figure out what is wrong with his car
- Resources to fix it
- Plenty of time to fix it

And, on top of all that, this man is stuck in a place right now where he can't leave yet anyway.

And even though what this man "should" do might seem obvious to you, there are obstacles that stand in his way.

The challenge he has isn't whether or not he should take the time to assess his car and fix what needs to be fixed, because it's obvious that the decision to fix the vehicle is the wise decision.

So here are the challenges he actually faces:

- In the place where he is, it's not "cool" to work on your car
- The people around him tell him that it's a sign of weakness to work on your car
- The people around him tell him just to keep blaming the road for why he can't make the trip

So real challenge he has is that, in the place where he's stuck right now, the people he surrounds himself with keep telling him that getting his car checked is "stupid." They don't want him to work on his car, so they tell him to just play childhood games, talk about people, blame everyone else for why they are where they are, and just keep doing the same things they've always done.

The people around this man don't want him to figure out and fix what's wrong with his car, because they know that they don't want to have to take the time and effort to fix their own cars. It's easier in that place to just complain about how things are and blame everyone else.

So now this man is faced with a choice: He can either take the time he has to work on his car or not. It's up to him. It's up everyone in that place to do the same, actually.

**Questions to Consider:**

1. How can you apply this story to you?

_____

_____

2. What kind of things do you see people around you doing instead of working on themselves (i.e., their "vehicle" to being free)?

_____

_____

3. What kind of things do you hear people around you say about people working on themselves? (i.e., "**Yes**, *that's okay to do*, **but** *until other people….*" etc.)

_____

_____

4. What advice would you honestly have for the man in this story?

_____

_____

5. Describe specifically how you are applying things from this workbook into your every day life:

_____

_____

*The same paths lead to the same destinations.*

# HERE'S HOW LIFE "SHOULD" BE

Since all of the information in this personal development is important to live out (not just do an exercise and move on, but really integrate into your life), it's important to review and strengthen ideas that you have already learned. In this exercise, you are building on what you learned about the Cartoon World/Real World. Remember, the bigger the gap between the way the world is and the way we think the world "should" be, the more dissatisfied we will be with life. It's natural to want the world to be a certain way or to think that things "should be" fair, but the reality is that life is the way it is, not the way we think it should be.

This exercise is designed for you to get an accurate picture of your "shoulds." In other words, it's very important for you to understand what demands you make of others and the world, even if those demands are only in your mind.

| Here's how life "should" be: | Here's how life actually is: |
|---|---|
| | |
| | |
| | |
| | |

*The more you can learn to "align your expectations with reality," the more prepared for it you'll be.*

# How Where I Grew Up Shapes Me

In general, young people who grow up in dangerous settings spend more time in survival mode than those who live in less threatening areas. Oftentimes, the first line of defense is to walk around being angry, because a person who looks really angry is less of an easy target than someone who might present as nice. There are, after all, unwritten survival codes or rules that people rarely talk about but always follow. Part of those codes are: The more aggressive you are, the less likely it is that others will be a threat to you.

Where you grow up shapes you, but it doesn't have to define you. The more you understand about how your past impacted you, the better chance you have to grow from that information. For example, some people are taught never to challenge those who helped them out in life. And even though it's easy to question authority figures and people you don't know, it can be really hard to question your in-group or those who have helped you out in life. But questioning things people taught you doesn't mean that you are questioning everything about them.

And it isn't disrespectful to question why you do the things you do in life or why people teach you certain things. In fact, anyone who doesn't want you to question what they tell you only wants to have complete control of you like a puppet. The truth is, you are the only one who can define you, and in order for you to define you, you have to know who you are and why you do what you do in life. Knowing yourself involves knowing how your past has shaped you so far.

1. How has where you grew up shaped you?

_____

_____

_____

_____

2. What can you question or challenge about where you grew up to help you break free of just following what you were taught growing up?

_____

_____

_____

_____

3. How does your current environment shape the way you move, the way you talk, the habits you have, and your goals?

_____

_____

_____

_____

_____

_____

_____

_____

*The more you can challenge even your own deeply held ideas, the more likely you are to build a solid foundation from which you can thrive in your life from this moment forward.*

# Size Does Matter

Your physical size (your height, weight, muscle mass, etc) all play a role in not only how you experience the world, but also in how others experience you. For example, a large man who stands overtop of his wife and screams at her but does not hit her might think, "She was never in danger because I knew I would never hit her." But his wife who is significantly smaller only saw his actions, not his intentions, and it would make perfect sense why that situation would be so intimidating and abusive.

To put this in perspective, imagine that an 8-foot-tall man who weighs 500lbs of solid muscle stood overtop of you yelling at you. He might not intend to hurt you, but what might go through your mind as this bigger person is standing overtop of you? Now, think of relationships you have and the size difference in them. This is why I have always taught men to sit down in disagreements with their wives. When two people are sitting down, it evens the playing field at least more than one person towering over another. Sitting down doesn't fix everything, but it is a step in the right direction. The point is that size impacts both your interactions and your attitude, and understanding that makes all the difference.

**The Big Guy**

Young men oftentimes think that being a bigger, stronger guy makes things easier, but as is the case with every person on the planet, there is always more to individuals' experiences than what others see. In the case of being a bigger, stronger kid, there often come challengers who want to prove they're tougher. That means that a big, strong kid who just wants to go about his day is all of a sudden thrust into a situation where he has to defend himself from an insecure threat to his safety. So now, instead of this young man focusing on whatever was on the agenda for his day, he now has to face a physical threat – and for no other reason than for the fact that his size intimidated the insecure kids who felt the need to challenge him.

Bigger guys, like everyone else on the planet, judge others by their actions but judge themselves by their intentions - and the reason that's worth understanding is that bigger guys might know that they have no intention of threatening someone else, but just by the nature of their size, they can most definitely intimidate others who are afraid of what the big guy "could" do if he got angry or lost control. So size not only impacts how big guys talk to others, it also impacts how others talk to them. Again, it's not wrong or bad to be big, this is only about understanding. It's about bringing awareness to the reality that size does impact communications.

## The Little Guy

Oftentimes, guys who are a little smaller when they grow up, grow up with what they feel is "more to prove." Guys who are smaller in stature, like everyone else on the planet, often feel the need to gain ground in areas where they see themselves falling short. This means that smaller guys can often lash out to prove that they are not afraid or unwilling. The results of this kind of attitude often land "the little guy" in hot water. Many times, guys who are smaller in stature will try to make up for their size with their attitude.

There is nothing wrong or bad about any size whatsoever, but there are certainly advantages and disadvantages to be mindful about when it comes to your physical size. Whether you are a smaller guy, or whether you're interacting with a smaller guy, it's important to understand that, just like with bigger guys, there is significantly more to people than their size.

**Challenge yourself to understand:**

1. How has your physical size affected your life (and the decisions you make)?

_____

_____

_____

_____

2. In what ways has your physical size played a role in your relationships?

_____

_____

_____

_____

Regardless of how big, small or medium your physical size, the fact is that your size impacts the way you see and experience the world (and the same is true for everyone else). There is no such thing as a "correct size" or even an "optimal size," but there certainly is such a thing as people understanding how their size *impacts* how they act and the decisions they make every day. The more you understand how your physical size impacts your interactions and attitude, the more control you have over your own life.

When it comes to understanding how your presence impacts others, size absolutely matters.

**Applying what you learn:**

1. How can you use this information on how your size has and will impact your interactions?

_____

_____

_____

_____

2. What kinds of things can you do to communicate effectively regardless of your physical size?

_____

_____

_____

_____

*Remember: People see your actions, not your intentions.*

# Advantages and Disadvantages

There are advantages and disadvantages in life. You have some advantages in some areas and some disadvantages in other areas. Life will never be completely fair, and it's not supposed to be. It's natural for people to downplay the advantages they have and highlight the disadvantages. On an individual level, understanding advantages and disadvantages impacts your personal growth being either accelerated (sped up) or stunted (slowed down).

On an interpersonal level, however, advantages and disadvantages can cause turmoil, because whereas individuals can be flexible with themselves regarding how they evaluate their advantages and disadvantages, when it comes to establishing consensus among multiple people regarding which advantages and disadvantages are "better" or "worse" than others, the challenge becomes immeasurable.

1. What **advantages** have you had throughout your life, and how have those advantages impacted your life?

_____

_____

_____

_____

2. What **disadvantages** have you had throughout your life, and how have those disadvantages impacted your life?

_____

_____

_____

_____

3. Did you write more for number 1 or number 2, and what do you think that says about you?

_____

_____

_____

_____

4. It's normal to emphasize the significance of the obstacles you face and downplay the obstacles that others face. Understanding that, **describe what it means for you to reflect on your advantages and disadvantages versus what it means for you to reflect on other people's advantages and disadvantages.**

_____

_____

_____

_____

*We have a tendency to highlight the advantages others have and downplay the disadvantages that they have, and we tend to highlight the disadvantages we face while downplaying the advantages we have.*

# Perspective

Sometimes being in a different position and seeing yourself through a different lens or from a different vantage point can give you profound insight. In this exercise, push yourself to see yourself from a different perspective.

1. With everything that you know, if you were your father, how would you advise yourself right now?

_____

_____

2. If you were your counselor, how would you guide yourself right now?

_____

_____

3. If you were able to be one of the walls in a prison cell that saw many prisoners live there, what perspective might you come to have?

_____

_____

4. If you were the warden of a prison you were in, how might you see you?

_____

_____

5. If you were a corrections officer (CO) and you didn't know you personally, what kind of impression do you think you would honestly make on you as a CO?

_____

_____

6. Imagine it's 50 years from now and you are still alive and able to look back on where you are right now. How do you see your situation differently?

_____

_____

_____

_____

7. Imagine you are so far in outer space that our sun only looks like a distant star. How does this perspective shift how you see your current situation?

_____

_____

_____

_____

*Remember that anytime you get stuck in your journey, you always have the ability to mentally step outside of yourself to give yourself a different perspective.*

# Seasons

The one overwhelming constant in life is change. Life can be broken up into seasons. If we think of life from age 1 to 100, then every 25 years can be thought of as a "season of life." In life, we often feel like more is expected of us than actually is. There are far fewer things expected of you than what it feels like. For example, in your first 25 years of life, you are expected to go to school, listen to guidance, graduate, and get a job. The more you break down what is actually expected of you, the more you'll be able to see how you are handling those expectations, as well as what you can do from this moment forward throughout the rest of the seasons of your life.

What types of things are expected or required of you in each of the following seasons of your life?

1.   Birth through age twenty-five:

| What was expected of me: | What I did / How I plan to meet or exceed those expectations: |
|---|---|
|  |  |

2.   25 years old to 50 years old:

| What was expected of me: | What I did / How I plan to meet or exceed those expectations: |
|---|---|
|  |  |

3.  From 50-75 years old:

| What was expected of me: | What I did / How I plan to meet or exceed those expectations: |
| --- | --- |
|  |  |

4.  After 75 years old:

| What was expected of me: | What I did / How I plan to meet or exceed those expectations: |
| --- | --- |
|  |  |

Society expects things from you. Your family expects things from you. Your loved ones expect things from you. You expect things from you. It's important to be mindful of what those expectations are, how they impact and shape you, and whether they are even worth trying to live up to.

1. Describe the kinds of outside expectations you've had on you, and how those expectations have impacted you:

_____

_____

_____

_____

2. Describe the way you have either lived up to the expectations of others or yourself:

_____

_____

_____

_____

3. Describe the healthiest expectations you can have for yourself from this moment forward:

_____

_____

_____

_____

*Align your expectations with reality.*

# Limited Time, Unlimited Options

There will be a beginning, middle and end to this day. There will be a beginning, middle and end to your current prison sentence. There is only a limited amount of time in every day, and there is only a limited amount of time that you will be incarcerated. Despite the limitations that time imposes, there are almost unlimited options for all the different ways you can spend your time.

Let's play out a few common ways to spend your time, so that you can at least consciously choose the path you want to take.

1.  **Complain as much as possible.** One option you can do is complain as much as you can about anything that is asked of you. You can say things like, "This is stupid!" or "Why should we have to do this?" or "How can these people know anything about us?" or "This has nothing to do with me." The psychology behind the personality who tends to complain a lot is filled with fear. A person who is filled with fear will talk more about how he should be doing anything other than what he's doing, and he does that in general because he's afraid that if he fully throws himself into what he's doing and doesn't succeed, then it would have been easier for him psychologically to just "not try," and then blame any lack of success on his lack of effort. This option is not wise, but it is an option.

2.  **Try to drag others around you down to set them up for failure when they leave**. Usually when people are really insecure, they choose this option. In this option, a person spends his time talking about how "dumb" everything is that is asked of him. Typically, people who choose this option try to be the "**class clown**," and they constantly look to others (usually their peers) for validation. For example, they might tell a joke and then look around to see who is laughing. They usually spend the majority of their effort trying to convince others to be as pessimistic as they are and talk about how "nothing works," because if they can convince others that the program they're in is "stupid," then they don't have to actually do any work themselves. The psychology of people who choose this option tends to also involve fear of failure, but it also includes a deep-seated belief that nothing can change. This option is also not wise, but it is also absolutely an option for you.

3. **Throw yourself fully into personal growth regardless of who is watching or what "credit" you get, and work as hard as you can.** In your entire life, you are the only person you will ever live with, and you are the only person who you can control. Those who pick this option understand that change is absolutely possible, but they also understand that change isn't easy, and it takes time. People who choose this option believe in themselves, or at least in their potential. They are capable, and they are not afraid of work. Like numbers 1 and 2 above, this action is also an option for you to choose.

In addition to these 3 common options that people tend to choose, there are also unlimited options that you can choose. In the space below, talk about the option that you seem to choose, and use examples of how your actions reflect your choices:

• How you use your time: _____

_____

_____

• What behaviors others see: _____

_____

_____

_____

_____

*When you actively manipulate others, you spend time trying to convince them to think of you a certain way. When you're working on yourself, you don't try to convince others of anything with your words, because you're too busy showing it with your actions.*

# THE WHOLE STORY

Four blind men were put around an elephant. The first felt the elephant's ear and remarked what a beautiful tapestry it must be. The second person felt the elephant's tail and said that the first man was certainly wrong, and that it was not a tapestry but a rope. The third man felt the elephant's leg and told the first two that they were way off, because they were obviously standing in front of a pillar. Finally, the fourth man touched the trunk of the elephant and remarked that they must be in front of snakes. Despite not being able to see, all four men were absolutely *certain* about what they experienced, and they believed with all of them that their experiences were the *complete truth*.

The four blind men went back to their respective towns and told others of their experience. The people in the towns supported what each blind man said. The people grew angry with the other men for being "wrong," and all four towns eventually grew to hate each other. The anger that the people felt in each of the towns grew, and the interesting thing was, the anger that each of them felt was built on people being "certain" about something that was wrong.

The four towns eventually went to war with each other, and the pain and hatred that ensued from years of war where many people suffered were all rooted in those four blind men's original experience, and the certainty that each of them felt regarding their experiences being absolutely complete.

The story of the four blind men and the elephant is one that we can all learn from, because we all have a tendency to be "certain" about what we know, even if we do not have all the details. People rarely take complete responsibility for their actions, especially when they mess up. *We all have a tendency to minimize what we do wrong*, whereas we have a tendency to maximize what others do wrong. We all, also, have a tendency to believe that the experiences we have are absolute truth, and worse, "complete" truth. But despite our egos trying to convince us that we have all the answers, the more accurate reality is that the only truth we ever really come to learn is partial (it's simply incomplete). So remember that when you hear a story about someone getting in trouble, you are not likely getting the entire story. And when you tell the story of you being in trouble, you are not likely telling the entire story.

We have all had the experience of feeling strongly about something only to learn later on that we were wrong about what we thought because we did not have the complete story. The next time you find yourself getting upset when you do not have the whole story, try to remember the story of the four blind men and the elephant.

**Putting what you know into practice:**

Tell the story of what led to you being incarcerated from four different perspectives.

_____

_____

_____

_____

_____

_____

_____

_____

_____

_____

_____

_____

_____

_____

_____

*Only the foolish believe their perspective is definitive.*

# Assessing How I Impact Those Around Me

What I bring to my housing unit and the people around me:

- **My energy level:**

    1    2    3    4    5    6    7    8    9    10
    Low                                             High

- **My attitude / Self-talk:**

    1    2    3    4    5    6    7    8    9    10
    Negative                                    Positive

- **The support I give to the people around me:**

    1    2    3    4    5    6    7    8    9    10
    Disconnected                            Easily observable

- **My ability to accept feedback from others (and learn from it):**

    1    2    3    4    5    6    7    8    9    10
    Closed off / Defensive                    Open / Willing

- **My work ethic (that others can visibly see me doing):**

    1    2    3    4    5    6    7    8    9    10
    No effort                               Everything I have

- **The amount of time I'm putting into working on myself (to lead others around me by example):**

    1    2    3    4    5    6    7    8    9    10
    Low                                   Nonstop

*Just as easily as you learn about others by watching their actions, others are learning about you by watching your actions, as well.*

# How We Interact with Others

There are different parts to all of us. In any given day, we experience different moods or states of being. Until we know ourselves really well, we are often moved from one state to another by others like we're some sort of puppet. For examples, if someone starts nagging at us enough, we will tend to get angry and lash back at them. In that sense, their "nagging" controlled us like a puppet, because it brought out of us a state or mood that we weren't in before that person began nagging.

When you can learn about the different states that you experience all the time, you can have a much better chance at being in control of yourself regardless of what others are saying or doing. Remember, the ultimate goal for all of us is to be able to be in such control of ourselves that no one can take away our sense of peace. This exercise is designed to help you get a better sense of the different types of states of mind we all experience.

This exercise is based on the work of Eric Berne, who created Transactional Analysis, which might sound complicated, but when we break it down, "transactional analysis" really just boils down to this: *trans* means *across*, *actions* are our *behaviors*, and *analysis* means to *evaluate*; so "transactional analysis" just means that we evaluate how our behaviors impact others, and how other people's behaviors impact us.

According to Eric Berne, there are 5 states that we operate out of:

**Nurturing Parent (NP)** = The compassionate, kind part of us (This is the state of mind we're in when we're just being kind or caring toward others. For example, the part of us that says, "I love you," or "I care about you.")

**Critical Parent (CP)** = The critical, demanding part of us (This is the selfish part of us that is angry with others for not being what we want them to be or doing what we want them to do. For example, "You should…" or "You better…!")

**Adult (A)** = The rational, level-headed part of us (The part of us that's able to recognize that even though a situation might be unfortunate, we can also recognize that it's not the end of the world.)

**Fun Child (FC)** = The part of us that just wants fun and just wants to do whatever it wants to do (i.e., our impulses)

**Hurt Child (HC)** = The part of us that feels sorry for ourselves (The part of us that might think or say, "It's not fair!")

The following questions will help you get a better picture of what your different states of mind might look like.

- When I'm in my Critical Parent (CP), these are the types of things that I tend to say and do:

_____

_____

- When I'm in my Nurturing Parent (NP), these are the types of things that I tend to say and do:

_____

_____

- When I'm in my Fun Child (FC), these are the types of things that I tend to say and do:

_____

_____

- When I'm in my Hurt Child (HC), these are the types of things that I tend to say and do:

_____

_____

- When I'm in my Adult (A), my outlook on situations mostly looks like this:

_____

_____

- I tend to operate mostly out of my (circle one) CP, NP, A, HC, FC

_____

_____

- What would your closest loved ones say that you need to work on the most?

_____

_____

**Applying What You Learn:**

1. Here is how this concept directly applies to me:

2. Here is how I have actually used this concept today:

*How you are impacts others, just as how others are impacts you: Challenge yourself to stay in your Adult Ego state as much as possible.*

# Radical Responsibility

Radical means "extreme," so the term radical responsibility refers to people taking extreme accountability for their actions. In this exercise, you are being challenged to take radical responsibility for everything in your life. Now remember, this is just an exercise, and you doing this exercise does not mean that you are actually responsible for everything that happens to you in life, but doing this exercise will help you be more accountable for absolutely every single thing that you do in life.

In other words, you are not responsible for what happens to you in life, but you are always responsible or accountable for what you do with what happens to you in life.

1. Describe your current situation, but do so from the perspective that you alone are responsible for every single aspect of what is going on in your life.

_____

_____

_____

_____

2. Describe the excuses that you have used in your life that really stopped you from challenging yourself the way you could have.

_____

_____

_____

_____

3. Describe what you can do starting today to catch yourself when you begin to make excuses or blame others for your actions.

_____

_____

_____

_____

The advantage to assuming complete responsibly for everything you say and do is that you alone actually are responsible for everything you say and do. But more than that, when you truly understand that you are the only one in control of what you say and do, you will work harder to focus on changing yourself, because no part of you will try to blame others for being how they are; instead, you will work to be the best version of yourself in the world in which you actually live, and you won't spend time in the cartoon world of how people "should" be.

Radical responsibility isn't just a concept for a class or a program, it's an actual way of life. The sooner you embrace it, the more control you begin to feel, because again, your only focus will be on the only person you can control (i.e., yourself), versus spending time trying to blame others for not doing what you want or being different from how they are.

*The greatest excuses in the world are still only excuses.*

# Treadmill

Once there was a mouse on a treadmill in his cage. Day after day he would run on the treadmill. From the outside, it seemed normal. After all, his cage was in a room with many other cages, and all had mice in them, and all the other mice did the same. I guess that's just what caged mice do. Or is it?

Something was wrong for this mouse. Something inside him told him there was more. Something told him that the standard way of living wasn't the ancient way of living, and so one day, he stepped off the treadmill. He just stepped off.

What would he do though? What was there to do? Well, there's no doubt that, in his cage, there were only so many places to go... And at first, like all other mice, he believed that.

That is, until he discovered a secret doorway to an incredible getaway: An entire universe that held unlimited space and endless knowledge. This mouse, you see, discovered his mind.

He no longer did the things he was supposed to do. When he saw other mice in other cages, he saw they did what they always did. They even would talk about him and tell him to get back on the treadmill. They hated being on the treadmill themselves, but it's what they were told to do: Not by those who put them in the cages, mind you, but by the other mice. The pressure mounted for this mouse to do what the other mice did, but this mouse was different. He just was. He always knew that, and so he went inward.

And every time the other mice mocked him and ridiculed him and laughed at him, instead of being offended, he felt pride. "I'm not like them, and with every bit of pressure they put on me, I see that more and more.

This mouse went so deeply within, that he began to trust what he discovered. For all his life he did what the mouse around him told him to do (he paid no mind to those who put them in the cages, because those who did that had nowhere near the same level of influence on him that the other mice did; and he knew he had to break free of their conditioning).

And day after day he sat in meditation; he sat in deep reflection. At first, he didn't know how to sit still. At first, he didn't know how to go inward, and the temptation from the outside grew strong: "Get back on the treadmill!" the other mice demanded. "That's so stupid!" they'd say. And if you really want to know the whole of this story - the hard truth of it - well, he almost listened to them. He almost quit.

But he held on.

And in one life-changing, generation-changing moment, everything shifted. What that little mouse discovered that day is immeasurably profound. It is so profound, in fact, that I cannot say it here; but even though I can't say what it was that changed, you can most certainly discover the answer for yourself.

"How?" you ask.

Get off whatever treadmill you're on. Go inward.

If you're like most, however, you will not pursue an answer. If you're like those other mice who laughed at and ridiculed the one who stopped doing what everyone around was doing, then you likely say that this too, is "stupid," and you'll likely say that as you're stepping onto the same treadmill you've always used. And that's okay too, because this story is for those who are strong enough to do something differently than those around them.

**Applying Your Understanding:**

1. What are some examples of psychological treadmills that you see others doing?

_____

_____

_____

2. What kinds of ways do the people around you try to pull you down and stop you from becoming the best version of yourself?

_____

_____

_____

*Knowing that rain is wet is not enough to keep you dry: You also have to do something about it.*

# How To Use Helpful Sayings and Powerful Passages

Only your actions will teach people if you have changed or are actually any different. Your actions alone are what others see, just as all you see of others is their actions. All too often, people say that they believe something, but their actions prove that they do not live out the things that they say they believe. The goal of this exercise is to help you increase the way your actions match your beliefs.

Write down some of the quotes or sayings that mean the most to you, and then describe how you either try or fall short of living out those sayings.

Quote:

_____

_____

How you either apply or try to apply that quote:

_____

_____

Quote:

_____

_____

How you either apply or try to apply that quote:

_____

_____

Quote:

_____

_____

How you either apply or try to apply that quote:

_____

_____

Passages are portions of written work – so you might find them in a book or an article.

1. What is one of the most helpful passages that you have ever read or learned?

_____

_____

_____

_____

2. In what ways have you relied on that passage in difficult times (if you haven't relied on it, then describe specifically how you could for the future)?

_____

_____

_____

_____

3. Speaking from a place of your own wisdom, what can you add to that passage?

_____

_____

_____

_____

4. What advice can you give yourself if you start to find that you are not following the advice that you know is best for you?

_____

_____

_____

_____

*The message that is lived by example is the most powerful one.*

# Disrespect

**Disrespect** – *To regard to treat with contempt or rudeness.*

People treat each other with contempt and rudeness all the time outside of prison, and for a lot of people, it's just not that big of a deal; but in prison, being disrespected is "unacceptable." In fact, many people who are incarcerated right now are locked up because they felt they were disrespected, and they felt they *had* to do something about it. Even in prison, men make decisions to spend years in the hole rather than be disrespected. Why? What is the measure of a man? Is the measure of a man how many people didn't disrespect him?

Many men in prison say that respect is all they have. Is that true? Is respect all any person has? If it's true that respect is all a person has, then the next question is: Why do people even want respect?

A lot of people equate respect with survival: "If others respect me, then I am safe, but if they disrespect me, then I am not safe." So out of fear that they will get hurt, some men go out of their way to make sure others don't disrespect them. Some men are willing to catch charges if someone disrespects them.

In reality, when a person goes out of his way to make sure others don't disrespect him, he only demonstrates that he is a puppet who is controlled by whether or not other people disrespect him. Seen through that lens, it seems like anyone who is someone else's puppet is really disrespecting himself. At the end of the day, however, how I or other people view respect is less important to your life than how *you view respect*.

It's possible that all people have a "line" that they will not allow to be crossed. For some people, that line extends so far out that they will not tolerate even being looked at the wrong way. For other people that line is very close. So the question for you is: What are you willing to sacrifice to avoid being disrespected?

> **A man who needs others to respect him is a servant to them. His entire worth and his actions are dependent on whether others do as he asks.**

In this exercise, the goal is to identify specifically what your line of disrespect is.

1. What does your line consist of? (In other words, what are the things that you consider so disrespectful that you will not tolerate them?)

_____

_____

2. What are you willing to give up to defend your line?

_____

_____

3. Describe a time in the past where you reacted strongly to being disrespected.

_____

_____

4. What consequences did you get for reacting so strongly?

_____

_____

5. Would you say that the consequences were worth you reacting as strongly as you did?

_____

_____

6. If the consequences weren't worth it, then what did you learn from the experience?

_____

_____

7. Do you believe it is possible for you to handle "being disrespected" differently? If so, how could you do it?

_____

_____

Many incarcerated individuals have told me in front of others that everything they did out of anger for being disrespected was worth it. But in over twenty years, and in sitting down with countless inmates, never once did anyone tell me, when it was just he and I in the room, that acting out of disrespect was ever worth it. The truth is that when others are around, it's important for most men to keep up the act that being disrespected is unacceptable and the worst possible thing; but it is also true that no one has the power to disrespect anyone if that person does not view the behavior as disrespect. Equally true is that no amount of any man's freedom is worth giving up simply because he was disrespected.

*"Free yourself from mental slavery. None but ourselves can free our minds."*
- Marcus Garvey
(and famously sung by Bob Marley in Redemption Song)

# Self-Evaluation: Checkpoint

One event led to another in the story of your life. This exercise is a checkpoint that's designed to help you assess where you are, how you got here, and what you can do to get to where you want to be. This is an opportunity for you to check where you are mentally, physically, and spiritually, as well as where you are literally.

1. I am in the mental space that I am in right now because:

_____

_____

2. The way for me to get in (or stay in) the best possible place mentally is by:

_____

_____

3. My body is in the physical shape it's in right now because:

_____

_____

4. The way for me to get in (or stay in) in the best possible physical shape is by:

_____

_____

5. I am in the spiritual place I'm in right now because:

_____

_____

6. The way for me to get in (or stay in) the best possible place spiritually is by:

_____

_____

7. Currently, I reside in:

_____

_____

8. What led me to living here is:

_____

_____

9. The type of excuses that will prevent me from getting to where I want to be mentally, physically spiritually or literally are:

_____

_____

10. The way for me to avoid allowing myself to make these excuses is by:

_____

_____

*Insight allows you to make changes in the fastest possible way.*

# The Basics of Change

This exercise is designed to get right to the heart of the matter. It doesn't matter if you've answered these or similar questions in the past, because these questions are meant to assess where you are *right now*.

1. What do you <u>want</u>?

   _____

   _____

2. What are you <u>doing</u> to help yourself get what you want?

   _____

   _____

3. Is what you are doing <u>working</u> for you? (If you say, "yes," describe how it is working for you.)

   _____

   _____

4. If what you are doing is not working, what <u>new approach</u> can you take to get what you want?

   _____

   _____

5. What <u>obstacles</u> seem to get in the way of your getting what you want?

   _____

   _____

6.  What can you do <u>to get around</u> those obstacles?

_____

_____

*If nothing changes, nothing changes.*

# Interacting with Others

Interacting with other people is a regular part of life. The more you learn about how you do it, the better chance you'll have to do so in the most effective way possible.

1.  How do you respond to others when they complain to you?

_____

_____

2.  How do you handle situations where people repeatedly nitpick everything you do?

_____

_____

3.  What is your approach to dealing with people who tend to argue everything you present to them?

_____

_____

4.  From your perspective, how can you most effectively handle people who refuse to accept responsibility for their actions?

_____

_____

5.  From your perspective, what is the best approach to take with someone who takes things personally that are not personal?

_____

_____

6. What is your approach to talking to people who play the victim role constantly?

_____

_____

7. How can you tell when you are engaging in playing the vicim yourself?

_____

_____

8. What feedback do others give you that has you feel more defensive?

_____

_____

9. What feedback do others give you that makes sense?

_____

_____

10. What do you do that makes other people shut down?

_____

_____

*You will always play a role in every interaction you have: Control what you can, let the rest go.*

# WHAT GOOD DO YOU OFFER THE WORLD?

*Once there was a man who lived in a state of darkness and was completely self-centered. He was just a mean person who would cuss people out and put others down. He complained about anything he could complain about. He blamed everyone else for his actions. In truth, he drained the life out of almost everyone who came into contact with him. He was imprisoned in his own mind because he was filled with hate, and he seemed to serve no good purpose at all.*

*One day this self-centered man met an old man. He complained to the old man. He put the old man down the moment the old man didn't see things his way. He cussed out the old man. He talked at him (not with him) until he actually tired himself out from talking. Finally, with at least one moment of silence, the old man had an opportunity to say something in rebuttal. Instead of saying a whole lot or preaching at this self-centered man, however, the old man simply looked at him in the eyes and asked, "What good do you offer the world?"*

What purpose is there to exist if there is nothing positive we can offer the world? Is the purpose to exist simply to spread hate and misery? There is no doubt that everybody makes mistakes, and there is no doubt that everyone has hurt people at times and also had times where they struggle. But there are some people who are struggling so much (like the man in the story above) that they only know how to be self-centered and hateful. Because these people are so filled with hatred, no one is really listening to them. Whatever they are angry about falls on deaf ears because they offer nothing kind. Unfortunately, instead of taking responsibility for themselves, self-centered people continually blame others for everything they can.

"Yes, but…" say the self-centered people, and then they go on to excuse why they do what they do. "Yes, but…" say the selfish people, and then they go on to minimize or downplay the harm they cause. But playing the "Yes, but" game only leads people to doing the same things they've always done and getting the same results they've always gotten.

To avoid becoming a self-centered person who lives in hate, ask yourself these questions in your mind, then answer number 1 in the space provided:

- *Do I spread a message of hope?*
- *Do I spread a message of hate?*
- *Do I encourage others to do good?*
- *Do I criticize (and then get defensive when others criticize me)?*
- *Do I antagonize others?*
- *Do I live a life right now with my actions that young people can emulate?*
- *What do people take away from being around me?*

1. What good do you offer the world?

_____

_____

_____

_____

_____

_____

*Those who feel sorry for themselves look to be reassured, those who understand that we all feel sorry for ourselves from time to time look to reassure others.*

# Who's Your "No"?

It's so easy to be skeptical of others, and it's even easier to be skeptical of those who think, feel, believe or behave differently from you. Being skeptical of others, however, is easy; but how skeptical are you of your own thoughts? How skeptical are you of the things that you feel certain about?

Celebrities, politicians, famous athletes, and the extreme rich are often surrounded by "yes people." Yes people are those who are afraid to challenge the main bread winner, which means that celebrities, athletes and the extreme rich who are in the public eye often find themselves in hot water for saying something out of touch with reality. One reason that is occurs because if everyone around you is telling you all your ideas and thoughts are great (i.e., "yes, people"), then it makes sense why you'd start to believe it. Celebrities, politicians, famous athletes, and the extreme rich who are in the spotlight need a "no" person in their lives to challenge them.

But so do you and I.

We all need a person (or several) in our lives who feels free to challenge us and challenge our ideas. But here's the tricky part: People who are good at telling others what they want to hear will say that they are willing to challenge them, but they simply don't. Regardless of what those in the public eye do, this is your personal growth quest, so the most important question right now is for you: Who's your "No" person?

If you don't have a "no" person, then you are much more likely to believe your own B.S.. So find a no person. Find someone to challenge you. Find someone who challenges even your most deeply held beliefs, because if you don't have someone to challenge you, then you are not likely to grow. If you hand pick that person and are calculated about the way you set it up, you can actually do more damage to your personal growth, because again, think about the celebrities, politicians, athletes, and extreme rich: They are told by those around them that they "are challenging" them. Reality says otherwise.

Here are guidelines for finding your "no" person:

- If a person just says "no" to say no then that person is likely just trapped in his own ego, and this is not a good challenge for you, because you will easily be able to tell that this person just says no to satisfy his own ego, and that won't likely help you much.

- If a person says they'll challenge you, but oddly never does because "everything you say just makes sense," then they are likely deceiving you. (Of

course, your ego will likely tell you it's because your ideas really are solid every time, so it makes sense why this person can't say "no.")
- If a person says "no" but can't offer thoughtful, insightful alternative perspectives, then again, this is not your "no" person.

If you have a "no" person, what deeply held thoughts, ideas and beliefs of yours have they challenged and changed your mind about?

_____

_____

_____

_____

_____

_____

If you don't have a "no" person, consider finding one. Until you find one in your personal life, it might be wise to talk to a professional counselor, social worker, psychologist, etc. (someone who has a professional responsibility to give you honest, direct feedback). That person can also help you find a "no" person in your personal life.

**Challenge your ego every step of the way.**

# Tattletale, Snitch, Whistleblower

Anyone who tells on someone for doing something wrong is a tattletale, snitch, or whistleblower. Whatever you call it, the concept is the same: "I want to do whatever I want, I don't want to have any negative consequences, and if someone tells on me for doing something wrong, I make that person the "bad guy."

Little kids who don't want to get in trouble threaten their brothers and sisters not to tell on them when they do things wrong. "Don't be a tattletale," they say. And when children do something wrong, they don't want others to find out, their best strategy, because they're too afraid to own up to their behaviors, is to make the "real problem" anyone who would tell on them.

In the street, people are threatened with being labeled a "snitch" if they tell on others for doing something wrong, and their faces are cut 150 stitches deep to remind them that no one is to be held accountable for their actions (ironically, the people who label those who "tell on" others are giving them negative consequences for their actions, but they are afraid to face their own negative consequences, so they make it all about those who are brave enough to call them on what they do wrong).

In the organizational world, a person who calls people on doing something wrong is called a "whistleblower." But like the little children and the people on the street, the concept is the same: Blast anyone who calls people on doing the wrong thing.

When did we get to the point that it's not okay to call someone on doing something wrong? And why do we, as adults, allow this behavior to continue?

If you would want someone to tell you who it was who hurt your children, then who are you to say that others who have their children hurt don't deserve to know who did it? If you would want to know who robbed your house, then who are you to say that others shouldn't have that same right to know? If you want people who do wrong things to you and your loved ones to be held accountable, then who are you to say that others don't deserve that same right?

The majority of this personal growth process deals with seeing things from multiple perspectives, and the same approach can be taken here. Let's look at "snitching" from the same, multiple perspective approach.

1. In the space below, argue for why people should never tell on others (i.e., snitch) for doing something wrong:

_____

_____

_____

_____

2. Now argue the same thing, except this time, make sure that you or your loved ones are the ones who were hurt, and use the same argument you used in number one to help the person who hurt you or your loved ones get away with no consequences:

_____

_____

_____

_____

3. Now argue for a different system altogether where adults are strong enough to be held accountable for their actions, and there is no longer such a thing as "snitching" or "whistleblowers" (and discuss whether or not you would still teach children to use the term "tattle-tale," or if you would teach them to be held accountable for their actions, too).

_____

_____

_____

_____

Once an incarcerated individual who was struggling with anger approached a teacher and demanded to know why COs don't call each other out when they see each other doing something wrong. The teacher agreed with the man that it's wrong to not call people out for doing something wrong. The man agreed.

Then the teacher looked at the floor for a moment, then looked back up at the man in front of him and said, "I agree that COs should call each other out when one of them does something wrong, I just also agree that inmates should do the same thing. But when was the last time you saw an inmate call another inmate out on something without either being labeled "snitch" or having his face cut open 150 stitches deep?"

And the man who was angry a moment ago stepped back and thought about what the teacher said. "You're right," he said. "We should. But we won't. I know I won't. So I guess that's why the COs don't."

But another man was standing there, and he jumped in the conversation and said, "Well they should have to. If they hurt us, they should be accountable." And the teacher asked, "And if you hurt them?" And the man said, "No, it don't work like that."

But then the first man who originally approached the teacher spoke up. He said, "Do you hear what we sound like? We want other people to do things we're not willing to do ourselves? That's the definition weakness, and I can't be for that."

# Journal of Transformation

_____

_____

_____

_____

_____

_____

_____

_____

_____

_____

_____

_____

# SELF-EVALUATION

People see your actions, not your intentions. Past behavior is the best predictor of future behavior. If nothing changes, nothing changes. At the end of the day, you are either different or you're not. Actions speak louder than words. The following exercise is designed to help you evaluate yourself as accurately as possible. The more accurate you are, the better chance you give yourself to grow as a person.

1. Describe how you use your free time.

_____

_____

2. Describe how you could use your free time more effectively.

_____

_____

3. What are some of the most important things that you have learned since you've been in prison?

_____

_____

4. How has what you've learned shaped the way you approach your every day?

_____

_____

5. What do people learn about you by watching your body language and listening to the tone of your voice? (In other words, how do you carry yourself, and how do others likely experience you?)

_____

_____

6. What do you think is most important for you to be successful on the outside?

_____

_____

7. What bothers you the most, and what do you do to handle it?

_____

_____

8. How does your self-talk impact your experience every day?

_____

_____

9. Give an example of a time you experienced conflict in prison and didn't handle it well:

_____

_____

10. Give an example of a time you experience conflict in prison and did handle it well:

_____

_____

11. Give an example of a time you acted on your impulses since you've been in prison:

_____

_____

12. Give an example of a time when you were able to resist your impulses since you were in prison.

_____

_____

13. Give an example of how you have specifically changed any of your beliefs since you've been incarcerated:

_____

_____

14. Give an example of how your communication on the phone was not reflective of your best self:

_____

_____

15. Give an example of a time when you specifically improved your communication on the phone since you've been in prison:

_____

_____

16. What bad habits are you trying to break currently (AND, what specifically are you doing to try to break those habits?

_____

_____

17. What books have you read (or videos have you watched) since you have been incarcerated that have impacted you (AND, how have you incorporated what you learned from those books/videos into your daily life)?

_____

_____

18. Give an example of a time when you have been selfish in the past:

_____

_____

19. Give an example of a time when you have been unselfish in the past:

_____

_____

20. Describe how would you evaluate yourself if it was entirely up to you to evaluate your growth and personal development:

_____

_____

_____

_____

_____

_____

_____

_____

*The more aware you are of how your thoughts impact you, how your actions impact others, and how you are impacted by others' actions, the more effectively you can pursue being the best version of yourself.*

# Insatiable

**Person 1:** "Why are you crying?"
**Person 2:** "I got a new shirt today."
**Person 1:** "But that's a happy thing, so why are you crying?"
**Person 2:** "Because it will get old one day."

A person who cannot breathe would do anything to be able to breathe. A person who cannot see would be grateful to be able to see. A person who cannot hear would be grateful to be able to hear. A person who is paralyzed would be grateful to be able to walk. A person who cannot speak would be grateful to be able to speak. A person who cannot read would be grateful to be able to read.

How many gifts do you have?

How many of your gifts, from your breath to your basic senses, to your ability to walk or read, do you honestly express gratitude for every single day?

It is possible to be grateful for what you have and still strive for more, but there is a difference in attitude between the person who is truly grateful and still striving for more and the person who takes his or her gifts for granted and still demands more.

What kind of person are you?

Not, what kind of person do you want other people to believe you are… but, what kind of person are you actually?

Are you like the person from the story above who cries about getting a new shirt, because you're thinking about how it won't be new in the future (i.e. it's not enough for you)?

Do you notice the little things that others do for you?

Do you appreciate when people even make an effort to help you meet your requests?

Or are you the kind of toxic, negative person who, regardless of what others do for you, remains negative and pessimistic and ungrateful for what you do have?

Challenge yourself to focus on what you do have rather than on what you don't have. Challenge yourself to show gratitude with your actions and with your attitude.

It's one thing to say that you don't like people who are entitled, but how many times have your actions reflected your own sense of entitlement? Remember the "Yes, but" game, too. Oftentimes, when we feel entitled, we really do believe that we are owed whatever we want, so we justify our entitlement with the "yes, but" game. BUT, that doesn't change the fact that entitlement is believing we are owed something (anything) that we don't currently have.

It's one thing to dislike entitlement; it's another thing entirely to not be entitled.

These next questions can be challenging for most people to answer, but do your best to push yourself to answer them honestly:

1. Describe a time when your sense of entitlement got the best of you:

2. Describe how you could have handled that situation differently, had you not felt so entitled at the time:

*The more you focus on what you have, from your breath to your basic needs, the closer you will be to peace.*

# From Anger & Ego to Growth: Self-Assessment

- **My anger:**

  1    2    3    4    5    6    7    8    9    10

  Needs work                           Complete control

- **My impulse control:**

  1    2    3    4    5    6    7    8    9    10

  Needs work                           Complete Control

- **My communication:**

  1    2    3    4    5    6    7    8    9    10

  Needs work                           Perfect

- **My ego:**

  1    2    3    4    5    6    7    8    9    10

  Needs work/understanding              Never an issue

- **My dedication to personal development:**

  1    2    3    4    5    6    7    8    9    10

  No effort                            Nonstop

Unless you marked a "10" on any of these, then you are acknowledging that you have more work to do around your personal growth. And that's great - because the reality is that you're human; and as long as you're alive, of course you will have more to work on every day... so do I, so does everyone.

Simply saying something like, "I know I have more to work on," however, is not enough, because those words ring hollow unless there is action behind them. This exercise is designed to have you first rank where you see yourself on each of those five areas (anger, impulse control, communication, ego, dedication to personal development), and then go deeper learning about how each one impacts your life.

**ANGER:**

Again, unless you marked a "10" (indicating that you have complete control over your anger), then you are acknowledging that you have more work to do. Simply saying, "I have more to work on," is not enough: instead it's important to identify specifically what you understand around your anger, as well as use examples to show how you apply what you learn.

**What have you learned so far in your life about how you experience anger?**

- What tends to trigger your anger the most?
- What is your typical response to anger?
- What do you do well around your anger?
- What do you struggle with most around anger?
- Give examples of times when you were able to apply what you know (or give examples of times when you were not able to apply what you learned):

**IMPULSE-CONTROL:**

It's important to identify specifically what you know about impulse-control, as well as use examples to show how you either practice or don't practice what you know.

**How has impulsivity (acting without thinking) impacted your life?**

- What areas in your life are most impacted by you *not* controlling your impulses?

- What does it feel like in your body when you have an impulse to do something?

- What thoughts go through your mind when you feel impulsive?

- What does it feel like after you have lost control or acted impulsively?

- How does your self-talk either help or hurt your sense of impulsivity?

**GETTING TO THE HEART OF YOUR COMMUNICATION:**

Having "perfect" communication is impossible, so of course we all have more to improve on when it comes to communication; but again, it's not enough to just say, "I have more to work on;" instead, it's important to identify specifically what you know about your communication, as well as use examples to show how you either practice or don't practice what you know.

**What have you learned through the years about how you communicate?**

- In what ways do you struggle with communication?
- How does your use of extreme words, such as *always* or *never* or *everyone* or *no one* impact the way you communicate?
- In what ways do you trigger defensiveness in others?
- What types of things do people say or do that get the strongest negative reaction from you?
- What specifically do you need to work on most around your communication, and what are you doing to work on it?

**UNDERSTANDING EGO:**

Your ego is your image of yourself. Oftentimes, we talk about ego as a synonym with pride. Your ego is that part of you that wants to be right about what you think or believe. The more you learn about yourself, the less defensive you become, and the more open you are to critically evaluate even your own thoughts and ideas.

**How has your ego caused you trouble throughout your life?**

- What does it mean to you to need to be right about what you think or believe?
- How does your ego get in the way of your personal growth?
- How does your ego impact your relationships?
- In what ways does your ego get checked by others?
- What specifically do you do to check your own ego?

**DEDICATION TO PERSONAL DEVELOPMENT:**

The more you want to learn about yourself, the more dedicated you become to growing in every area of your life.

**How have you grown psychologically throughout your life?**

- Talk about some of the books you have read that have impacted you.

_____

_____

- Describe some of the stories or experiences that you've encountered in your life that have shaped you.

_____

_____

- Talk about what it is that you want to learn about yourself the most.

_____

_____

- Talk about what you are actively doing to grow as an individual.

_____

_____

- What daily habits do you practice that help you with personal development?

_____

_____

- Describe your most recent personal growth experience.

_____

_____

- Describe what your biggest obstacles to personal growth are, and then talk about what you are actually working on to get around those obstacles.

---

---

This is what I am taking from this exercise:

---

---

---

---

*Anyone can say, "I'm not right all the time" or "I still have more to learn," but how many people can actually admit that they're wrong in the moment or when they're being challenged to question their own perspective?*

# Magnify & Personalize

When we're suffering on the inside, we have a tendency to do two things: **Magnify** and **personalize**. To magnify is to make something bigger than it needs to be. To personalize something is to take something personal that's not personal.

There are situations that we make bigger than they are, and there are things that we take personally that simply aren't personal.

**Magnifying:**

We magnify events with the language we use to describe them. For example, if someone says something to you, and you describe what they say with adjectives like, "She keeps *coming at me* with…" or "He keeps *throwing in my face* that…" those are examples of magnifying a situation. If someone is "coming at you," then that literally means they are moving forward toward you. For that statement to be accurate, a person would have to be continually moving toward you and closing in on you; otherwise, saying that someone is "coming at you," is an exaggeration and an example of magnifying. Similarly, if you use a statement like, "She's throwing that in my face," that is also an example of magnifying. Again, in order for that statement to be accurate, a person would have to be literally throwing something at your face.

When you magnify a situation, you make yourself much angrier than you need to be, and it makes sense why. The more you feel like you need to physically protect yourself, the more likely you are to react angrily. The problem with magnifying is that it makes you feel unnecessarily defensive. Unless someone is continually physically coming straight toward you or literally throwing objects at your face, the reality is that you are magnifying the situation by describing it that way.

**Personalizing:**

Everyone struggles. There have been times in your life when you were struggling and you took it out on others, even though those others didn't deserve you doing that. In those moments, it would have benefitted others to not take the pain you were feeling personally. In the same way, it's important for you to not take other people's pain personally. Displacement occurs when you "displace" (or put) anger or pain from one area of your life onto a completely different area. So, if you are angry or hurt by one person, but you take it out on someone else, then you are displacing your feelings. Everyone displaces from time to time.

When others lash out at you, it's important to step back and recognize that it is highly likely that their pain is not personal toward you, even if it seems or feels like it is. We can only ever give others what is inside of us, and others can only ever give us what is inside of them. In other words, if others are hurting inside, they might give us that hurt or take that hurt out on us (unfairly), and it's important to understand that their pain is not personal to us. Specifically, other people's pain is not personal toward you.

The fact that you have magnified and personalized situations in your life is completely normal. All of us have done that from time to time. The goal is to become aware of when you are magnifying or personalizing, because the more aware you are of when you do it, the better chance you have at not doing it.

- Give an example of a time when you magnified a situation that didn't need to be magnified:

_____

_____

- What types of words or phrases did you use to make that situation bigger than it needed to be?

_____

_____

- Give an example of a time when you took other people's pain personally:

_____

_____

- What can you do differently to avoid taking other people's pain personally in the future?

_____

_____

There's a difference between just saying, "Don't take things personally," and actually not taking things personally. It's easy to say the words, "Don't take things personally," but to really be able to avoid taking things personally takes effort. The more you realize that **people who are in a place of peace themselves would never hurt others**, the more it makes sense that the only people who ever hurt others are those who are hurting themselves, and that rings true for you and me, as well.

If you don't want others to take the pain you cause them personally, because maybe you know that you had a whole lot more going on inside your mind than what others could see and you didn't "mean it" – then please know the same is true for when others say and do things that are hurtful toward you: They only do so because they are struggling themselves. The more you truly realize that **only hurt people hurt people**, the less personally you ever take others' pain again.


• Give an example of a time when someone did something hurtful toward you:

_____

_____


• Now describe why that person might have done what he or she did from his/her perspective:

_____

_____


• Finally, from a neutral observer, describe exactly what happened using only accurate language:

_____

_____


***The more you step back and see others' behaviors through the lens of their perspective and with accurate language, the less you will magnify and personalize.***

# Mastering What You Practice

You will master whatever you practice in life. If you practice playing the piano, you will master that. If you practice swimming, you will master that. If you practice acting on your impulses, you will get very good at that, too. BUT, and this is important to know: If you practice peace, you will eventually master that.

1. Give an example of a time when you practiced snapping at others impulsively in anger.

_____

_____

2. Give an example of a time when you practiced a skill in your life.

_____

_____

3. Give an example of a time when you practiced a good habit (and what the result of that was).

_____

_____

4. Give an example of a behavior that you got good at doing even though you didn't want to (for example, complaining, blaming, acting impulsively, etc.):

_____

_____

5. Give an example of something that you wanted to get good at but just never took the time to really master it:

_____

_____

6.  List something in the space below that you want to master in life.

_____

_____

7.  What is something you can do every single day to help you practice getting good at what you wrote for number 6?

_____

_____

*Whether it's doing something you're proud to be doing, or whether it's doing something that you're not proud of at all, one thing holds true regardless: You will get better at anything that you actually do today.*

# It's NOT Us!

Everyone on the planet has issues. Everyone on the planet can improve. No one is perfect. Despite this fact, our ego convinces us that we are right about whatever we think, and even if we do ever acknowledge that we make mistakes, our ego tells us that our mistakes aren't *as bad* as the mistakes that others make. And our ego stops us from changing.

It gets worse in groups.

When like-minded people come together in groups, the feeling that they do everything correctly is amplified. The ego of the group is strong, because it's reinforced by its members. The group spends so much energy focusing on how *those who think or act differently from them are wrong,* that they reinforce their members' belief that they are right, and others are wrong. And the group ego stops people from changing.

How groups tend to acknowledge flaws and mistakes:

If groups do acknowledge flaws and mistakes, it is primarily through the lens of "Yes, but…." In other words, groups or group members might acknowledge briefly that they have things to work on, but then they are quick to minimize what they need to do differently, and fast to follow that up with *how those who oppose them have more to work on*. And then the group and its individual members collectively focus their energy as a group around how others *should* change. And the group ego reinforces each individual group member's ego. And that "Yes but" game stops people from changing.

So what *can* be done?

Each individual person can assume complete responsibility for him or herself. Each individual can focus on changing the only controllable in the world he or she can control himself or herself.

But what *will* be done?

Egos will drive people to keep saying, "It's not us!" And they won't likely change. Egos will drive people to say, "Yes I know I have things to work on, but what others have to work on is more…" and they won't likely change. Egos will continue to minimize what they do, and maximize what others do. And nothing will likely change…. Unless….

Maybe people will read this and understand it: and then things *will* change.

The real question is - without looking to the group in any way - **What will you do?**

**Questions to consider:**

1. In what ways do you challenge the groups with which you identify?

_____

_____

2. In what ways do you question your own in-group when conflict with others comes up?

_____

_____

3. In what ways do you stand up to your own group and confront them on being off base?

_____

_____

4. In what ways do you sometimes go with your in-group, even though a part of you wants to challenge what they are saying or doing and go in a different direction?

_____

_____

# The New Day Movement

Across the country, nearly 7 out of 10 inmates who leave prison eventually return to prison. That number of people coming back to prison is not okay. We must work to change that. The New Day Movement is a "state of emergency," whereby every person who is involved in prisons is now being called to take immediate action. The New Day Movement has begun. It is up to each of us to assume complete and total responsibility for every single thing we say and do. This is a brief overview of what this new movement is about.

The entire focus of the New Day Movement is rooted in what each of us can do to contribute to a better system.

---

**The Monk and the Mirror**

Once there was a monk who carried a pocket mirror with him everywhere he went. One day, a woman came up to this monk and said, "I thought you were supposed to be holy and humble. Instead, I see you checking yourself out in that mirror all day." To which the monk pulled out his mirror and replied, "Oh, this? Yes, I carry this with me wherever I go. You see, whenever I encounter troubles, I pull this mirror out to remind myself that I am both the source and the solution to my problems."

---

The New Day Movement is based on 3 primary goals:

**Inner peace**
**Education**
**Legacy**

### Inner Peace

If you've ever sat with others in hospice, then you likely understand that in people's final moments of life, they are not reminiscing about wanting to have gotten over on others more (or have gotten away with doing the wrong things); instead, in their final moments, people overwhelmingly now focus solely on peace.

And here's the lesson: You and I will one day have our final moment. And in that final moment, we will also likely only hope for peace. And as life has taught us so far: We will master whatever we practice. So if we want to have peace, we have to practice peace. And waiting until our final moment to start practicing peace will be too late.

So what can we do?

We can begin to practice peace. The New Day Movement is centered entirely on helping both ourselves and others find peace. Every day, every hour, every moment is an opportunity to practice living in the way that will bring us peace.

Practicing peace means staying in control of ourselves even when others are struggling and say and do things that are not reflective of their best selves. We all have a tendency to judge others harshly for the same things that we want to be judged easily on, and the more aware we are, the more we will be ready to change that.

In supporting your journey to inner peace, we will address:

- How what you say to yourself shapes how you experience the world
- How ego and the "need to be right" gets in the way of peace
- How to live from essence over ego
- How to be an example with your words and actions all the time

*"Be mindful that the energy you give the world is reflective of the best version of you."*

## Education

The word "education" literally comes from the root *"ed"* (also, *ex*) or *"out,"* and *"ducere"* or 'to lead.' So the word education literally means *"to lead out of…."*

To lead out of what? Darkness? Not knowing (i.e., ignorance)? If that is the case, then book-knowledge, as well as hands-on knowledge on life, is what matters most. To that end, every day of our lives must be devoted to spending at least some time to learning something new.

In addition to book knowledge, or knowledge about our world, knowledge about ourselves is incredibly important. The more personal growth we experience, the more effectively we handle whatever comes our way.

The New Day Movement is rooted in helping individuals pursue personal growth, and the focus is centered on each of us taking an honest look at how others are perceiving us. In other words, people see our actions, not our intentions, and whereas others judge us by our actions, while we judge ourselves by our intentions, the reality is that we also judge others by their actions, not by their intentions. When we become aware that it doesn't ever matter what we "meant to do" or "didn't mean to do" in life, then we can own complete responsibility for our actions. The more we focus on accepting complete responsibility for everything we think, feel, say and do, the better chance we have at changing any aspect that we need to change.

The New Day Movement Education is primarily centered on providing hands-on information about how we tend to handle life. To help you along the way with education, we will address:

- How we handle anger
- How we handle decision-making
- How we handle emotions
- How we handle relationships
- How we handle money
- How we handle life

*"Education is our pathway to helping us understand both our infinite outer and inner worlds."*

**Legacy**

The past is gone, the future is yet unwritten, and the present moment is the only time in which we can actually do anything. As long as we are alive, we have an opportunity to shape our legacy. Our legacy is not only about what we've done already, it is about what we are about to do, too, every waking moment, for the rest of our lives. The New Day Movement is intent on helping individuals create a legacy that aligns with the best version of themselves.

When we identify what legacy we want to leave, our next step is to figure out what obstacles stand in our way. Then, and this is the most important step, we need to figure out how to get around those obstacles so that we can pursue the best possible path for ourselves.

The question to ask yourself is: *What content do you add to the world every day?* From the moment you wake up until the moment you go to sleep, every word you speak and every action you take counts toward the legacy that you're creating.

To help you pursue your legacy, it's important to address:

- How to recognize and act on the reality that people see your actions, not your intentions
- What obstacles can stand in the way of becoming the best version of yourself, AND how to get around those obstacles
- A plan for impacting people in a positive way
- A goal (and plan) for sustainability

*"Today counts toward your legacy."*

There is a difference between what you *mean* to contribute to the world today and what you *actually* contribute. The more clearly you can see the difference between the two, the faster you can figure out what it is you need to work on the most. Life isn't about getting over on others or fooling people, it's about living authentically and leaving behind a legacy that tells an accurate story of the life you led.

The words you speak matter more than the ones you "meant to say."
The actions you take matter more than the ones you "meant to do."

You are the ONLY person with complete and unrestricted access to your mind. You and you alone know whether or not you live in complete peace in your mind. To take accurate accountability for what goes on in your own mind (again, remember that you are the only one in control of what gets focused on in your mind), it's important to be accurate about what you actually thought, said and did today.

- This was the focus of my thoughts today:

_____

_____

- This is how the words I spoke today impacted others:

_____

_____

- This is how my actions today impacted others:

_____

_____

Your legacy is NOT about what you "meant to do" or how you "meant to be" while you were incarcerated, and it's certainly not about how many classes you took, but instead, it's about seeing the actual behavioral changes you've made.

Even though it's very natural for other incarcerated individuals to try to convince you that "all you need to do is say the right thing that they need to hear," the fact is, those who try to tell you that are wrong. Both mental and physical prison isn't about learning new ways to "try to convince" others that you're different; it's about *actually becoming different*. It's about learning and growing, and it's about becoming the kind of person who lives his life by things like inner peace, education and legacy.

That is why this movement isn't about what you can just tell others: ***It's about what you can actually be for the world***.

• How I will work on inner peace today:

_____

_____

• How I will work on education today:

_____

_____

• How I will work on my legacy today:

_____

_____

*You will not be defined by what you meant to say or do in life:*
*You will be defined by what you actually say and do.*

# Self-Inventory:

- This is the kind of person I was before I was incarcerated:

_____

_____

- This is the kind of person I was early on in my incarceration:

_____

_____

- This is the kind of person I have been recently:

_____

_____

- This is what the words that I speak out loud actually teach others about who I am:

_____

_____

- This is what the actions that I take actually show others about who I am:

_____

_____

- This is an example of how I used to minimize the things I did:

_____

_____

- This is an example of how I have grown to take complete responsibility for what I do:

_____

_____

- If you listened to me and watched me before I was incarcerated, and if you compared that to how I speak and act now, here are the differences that you would likely see (and here are behavioral examples to help illustrate those changes):

_____

_____

_____

_____

To be a part of the New Day Movement all you have to do is go inward and pursue learning about yourself constantly. If you have ideas on ways that you can spread awareness and support to others around inner peace, education and legacy, please reach out to others and find ways to initiate the kinds of changes or support that you'd like to see. Remember, the entire movement is about those who suggest new ideas actually living out those ideas, so at no point is this movement about "telling others" what they "need to change;" instead the focus of everyone involved in the New Day Movement is on ourselves and what each of us can do differently to constantly improve. The goal is to be a little bit better every single day.

# Reality Check:
# Taking Control of Your 168 / 10,080

There are 168 hours (or 10,080 minutes) in a week. How you spend your time is more reflective of what you really want in life than what you *say* you want. So, the question is: how do you spend your 10,080 minutes each week?

- How many of your minutes do you spend complaining every week?

- How many of your minutes each week do you spend reading something that challenges you?

- How many of your minutes each week do you spend talking like a teenager (i.e., using exaggerated language, talking smack on others, complaining about things not being "fair," etc)?

- How many of your minutes do you spend each week trying to convince others that you're right about something?

- How many of your minutes do you spend having arguments in your head?

- How many of your minutes do you spend being reactive to what others say or do?

- How many of your minutes do you spend practicing a skill that you want to master?

- How many of your minutes do you spend thinking about the *unchangeable past* rather than focusing on the very real present?

- How many of your minutes do you devote to learning more about yourself?

- How many of your minutes each week do you spend on making a positive impact on others or leaving a positive legacy to the world?

You are the only one who knows exactly how many of your minutes you spend dwelling in negativity in your mind, or how many minutes you spend focusing on what you can change, what you have control over, and what you are doing to leave a positive legacy to the world. **You are the only one who lives inside your mind.** Give yourself a reality check be honest with yourself. If you don't like how many minutes you spend on things like negativity, playing the yes but game, or waiting for others to be how you want them to be before you take complete responsibility for your thoughts, words and actions dash then change it.

**Take control of your 168**. Map out how you spent the last 10,080 minutes of your life (even in your own mind) - and then map out a plan for how you'll spend the next 10,080 minutes of your life.

Give yourself an honest assessment. Do NOT allow yourself to make excuses. Have the courage to challenge yourself to be the best version of you. Have the courage to live your next 10,080 minutes in the best possible way for you.

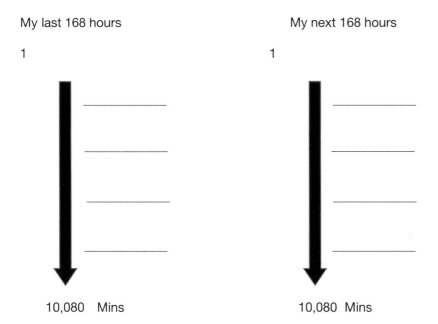

My last 168 hours

1

_____

_____

_____

_____

10,080  Mins

My next 168 hours

1

_____

_____

_____

_____

10,080  Mins

*You are the only one who lives inside your mind: How you spend your mental time is entirely up to you. Until your inner world is in complete peace, there is more work to be done.*

# How I Am Different

You have spent the last 21 days with the opportunity to go inward in a deeply reflective way. You have had the opportunity to be mindful of the thoughts that go through your mind (that is, to be aware of your self-talk). You have seen the phrase "people see your actions, not your intentions," over and over again, and you have had the opportunity to use that statement to impact your own behavior.

You have also had the opportunity to fully dive into setting clear goals, identifying clear obstacles, and work to learn new ways to help you be successful in every area of your life.

Your inner dialogue throughout these past 21 days was entirely up to you. You are now at the end of this program, and the question you were told this program was based on is now being asked of you:

• Who have you become?

_____

_____

_____

_____

• Who are you becoming?

_____

_____

_____

_____

- How are you different now than you were 21 days ago?

_____

_____

- What is your plan for when you re-enter society?

_____

_____

- What do you still have to work on the most?

_____

_____

- What have you done really well with over the last 21 days?

_____

_____

- What have you struggled with the most over the last 21 days?

_____

_____

- What part of your actions do you blame others for?

_____

_____

- What is one of the most important things that you've learned about yourself over the last 21 days?

_____

_____

- What is one of the most important things that you hope to learn about yourself moving forward?

_____

_____

- What questions do you think are the most important to ask about you?

_____

_____

- What is the best possible plan that can help you take full advantage of the rest of the time you have to train (i.e., the rest of the time you are incarcerated)?

_____

_____

*You will only ever live with you your entire life; so it's wise to get to know yourself.*

# Please climb

Once a Zen master told two of his disciples about a legendary tree of five fruits on the other side of the great mountain, so the two students set out to find it. At one point, when they sat down to rest, the one student (who was understandably tired and afraid) said, *"The mountain is too high, I know I can't make it,"* and he gave up, so he laid down to sleep. The other student, who was also very tired and scared, kept going anyway, and somehow, some way, he made it to the tree of five fruits.

On his way back home, he came across the other student who had sadly frozen to death in the night. When the student came back to their teacher he said, *"Maybe my companion would have lived if tried to scale the mountain, because at least he would have been warm from moving; but even if it was his fate to die, I think it would have been better for him to die trying...."*

And that is the lesson for me – because I don't know what you or I will ever accomplish when we set out to do what we want to do in life; but I do know exactly what both of us will get if either one of us decides to give up.

No matter what it ever feels like. No matter where you ever are: Please climb, because you are stronger than you realize, and you are absolutely worth your effort.

*The only person who can limit you is you.*

# Lightbulb

**(Adapted from the book, *Life Lessons*)**

Thomas Edison worked hard to develop the lightbulb. Legend has it that when the first working version was finally completed, Edison handed it to a boy who was in his lab, and he told the young man to take it upstairs. Along the way the boy tripped, fell, dropped the light bulb, and broke it. It is said that Edison, vexed as he might have been on the outside, went right back to work making another one without complaining. In 24 hours, Thomas Edison had created the lightbulb again. The moment this next version was completed, he looked at the very same boy in the eyes, and again handed him the lightbulb.

Edison likely knew that something much bigger was at stake for this young man.

People make mistakes. People actually make lots of mistakes. So do you. So do I. Sometimes we learn from our mistakes; sometimes we're still in the process of learning. Handing the lightbulb back was a symbol of kindness, understanding, forgiveness, and love. Is there someone in your life that you need to hand lightbulb to today?

How about to yourself? It is time for you to rebuild a new lightbulb, and then have the confidence to give that newly built lightbulb back to yourself.

Mistakes are an inevitable part of life; everybody makes mistakes – but only the wise learn from those mistakes.

Push yourself to learn from every moment, and then work hard to be able to communicate *how* you are changing to others. The "new lightbulb" that you're building *consists of your actions*; and the light that you will shine on the world is the light that you are creating by looking inward and focusing entirely on what you can control (i.e., yourself), and on what you can give the world (i.e., all your gifts, etc.).

**Be the light.**

# A Small Amount is a Lot

An incarcerated individual who was convicted of drug charges once sat in a prison group and said, "When I get out, I can't work for minimum wage… I have to go back to selling drugs because I have to provide for my family." Another, older and wiser peer of his said, "You think you have to provide for your wife by selling drugs, but let me ask you, 'is she making it on the outside right now without your help?" And the other man said, "Yes." So the wiser inmate continued. He said, "How much would an extra thousand dollars a month help your wife right now?" And the other man said, "Oh that would mean the world to her. Honestly, it would make her life so much better." To which his elder replied, "That's what you working an absolute minimum wage job would bring to her…. and more than that, you would actually be there for her physically by her side instead of locked up in here…."

And all of that? Well that's a fact.

Sometimes we think we need to do major things, when minor things will change everything.

### Vision. Hard work. Patience.

Be clear about what you want. Identify the path. Identify the obstacles. Train your body, mind and spirit to be the best possible version of yourself, and then work harder than anyone who's ever come before you. Once you have a vision, make it clear, and then work insatiably hard toward it, the final piece is patience. The more you cultivate patience, the better you get at it.

*Do the little things right, and before you know it, all the biggest things will be created.*

# 21 Days

At the onset of this 21 days, you were in a spot. Depending on the effort you put into the last 21 days, you are potentially in a vastly different spot. Like a snake that sheds its skin, the more effort you put into insight and making literal behavioral changes in your life, the more you shed who you used to be, and the closer you get to being the best version of yourself.

The question to ask yourself now is - after 21 days: Who have you become?

_____

_____

_____

_____

_____

_____

Whomever you have become, it will be wise to remember that the world will never see who you "meant" or "didn't mean to" become; they will only ever see who you actually are. And hopefully now, more than ever, you understand that people see your actions, not your intentions. Hopefully now, more than ever, you understand that every emotional experience you ever have will have a beginning, middle and end, that your emotions will come and go, but that your actions, what you actually say and do in this life, can never be erased.

***Who you are can impact the entire world.***

# Recommended Study

**Walking Through Anger: A New Design for Confronting Conflict in an Emotionally Charged World.** By Dr. Christian Conte

**Life Lessons.** By Dr. Christian Conte

**Teaching Stories: 53 Bits of Advice, Random Ideas, & Half-Told Tales to Contemplate & Spark Personal Growth.** By Dr. Christian Conte

**Zen Parent, Zen Child.** By Dr. Christian Conte

**Advanced Techniques for Counseling and Psychotherapy.** By Dr. Christian Conte

**The Art of Verbal Aikido.** By Dr. Christian Conte

**Mastering What You Practice.** By Dr. Christian Conte

**Getting Control of Yourself: Anger Management Tools and Techniques.** By Dr. Christian Conte (VIDEO)

**Rage.** By Ron Potter-Efron

**YouTube.com/DrChristianConte**

**Website: www.DrChristianConte**

**Podcasts:**
- **Tackling Life with Ray Lewis and Dr. Christian Conte** (iTunes, and anywhere podcasts are hosted)
- **Emotional Management** (iTunes, and anywhere podcasts are hosted)

*Sending everyone who reads this book, and everyone who doesn't, much peace.*

- Dr. Christian Conte

# ABOUT THE AUTHOR

Dr. Christian Conte is a Licensed Professional Counselor and level 5 Anger Management Specialist (highest level). He is the author of 8 books, including *Walking Through Anger,* widely recognized as a leading book in the field of anger management. Dr. Conte is the creator of Yield Theory, an evidence-based approach to communication rooted in compassion and conscious education. He has more than 20 years and 20,000 hours of clinical counseling experience working with people from all over the world. He is the co-host of the podcast Tackling Life with Ray Lewis and Dr. Conte, and the host of the podcast Emotional Management, heard on over 400 radio stations daily, including some Sirius XM stations. Dr. Conte is devoted to leaving a legacy of peace.

Made in the USA
Monee, IL
25 August 2024

64508832R00125